DAVE PELZ'S PUTTING GAMES

DAVE PELZ'S PUTTING GAMES

The More You Play, the Better You Putt

DAVE PELZ

WITH EDDIE PELZ

GOTHAM
BOOKS

GOTHAM BOOKS
Published by Penguin Group (USA) Inc.
375 Hudson Street, New York, New York 10014, U.S.A.
Penguin Group (Canada), 90 Eglinton Avenue East, Suite 700, Toronto, Ontario M4P 2Y3, Canada (a division of
Pearson Penguin Canada Inc.); Penguin Books Ltd, 80 Strand, London WC2R 0RL, England; Penguin Ireland,
25 St Stephen's Green, Dublin 2, Ireland (a division of Penguin Books Ltd); Penguin Group (Australia),
250 Camberwell Road, Camberwell, Victoria 3124, Australia (a division of Pearson Australia Group Pty Ltd);
Penguin Books India Pvt Ltd, 11 Community Centre, Panchsheel Park, New Delhi–110 017, India; Penguin Group (NZ),
67 Apollo Drive, Rosedale, Auckland 0632, New Zealand (a division of Pearson New Zealand Ltd); Penguin Books (South Africa)
(Pty) Ltd, 24 Sturdee Avenue, Rosebank, Johannesburg 2196, South Africa

Penguin Books Ltd, Registered Offices: 80 Strand, London WC2R 0RL, England

Published by Gotham Books, a member of Penguin Group (USA) Inc.

First printing, September 2012
10 9 8 7 6 5 4 3 2 1

All photos courtesy of Pelz Golf Institute, Eddie Pelz, and Sven Nilson.

LIBRARY OF CONGRESS CATALOGING-IN-PUBLICATION DATA
Pelz, Dave.
 Dave Pelz's putting games : the more you play, the better you putt / Dave Pelz with Eddie Pelz.
    p. cm.
 ISBN 978-1-59240-770-5
 1. Putting (Golf) I. Pelz, Eddie. II. Title.
 GV979.P8P44 2012
 796.35235—dc23
                    2012018365

Printed in the United States of America
Set in Sabon, Foundry Gridnik, and Meta
Designed by BTDNYC

To my girls, Laura Kay and Katherine Lynn,
the best daughters ever. I know I didn't turn out
perfectly, but you raised me the best way
you knew how, and for that I thank you.
I love you both so very much!

Fun

If practice is convenient and fun, is it really practice?

This book is about putting games: how to set them up and how to play them, so that you can have fun and improve your putting skills at the same time. And after playing them, your improved putting skills will transfer to the golf course with you!

The old adage that to improve your putting you must putt on the practice green until your hands bleed or your back breaks is herein replaced with a new motto: Play putting games in the convenience of your home during the week—and then putt better and shoot lower scores on the weekend.

I'm not selling false hope, a magic putter that can't miss, or suggesting that you can "buy" better putting. I'm simply saying that if you play these games, your putting skills will improve, and I'm also saying that improving your putting skills is the only real and long-lasting way to improve your putting.

What Will This Book Do for You?

It will give you:

1. Games to measure and evaluate your performance in seven areas of putting;
2. Games to improve your putting stroke mechanics; and
3. Games to optimize your putting touch and feel.

Many of these games can be played at home, and if you play them periodically, your putting will improve. The more you play them, the better you'll putt. And if you play them carefully—if you set them up properly and follow the rules—you'll optimize your improvement.

Even if you play each game only once, you'll at the very least become more aware of the skills critical to good putting, and the areas in which your skills are deficient. And for as long as you play golf, these games will always be there for you: to help you make more putts, shoot lower scores, and reduce your handicap.

Please Read This Book and Open Your Mind

You *can* improve your putting—*and* have fun doing it. First learn where your putting is weak and how to improve in that area of weakness, and then spend some time playing fun games to actually improve those skills. With just a little effort you'll experience measurably improved putting, and there's *no limit* to how good your putting can get!

The good news: Putting games are fun, they don't take too much time, and you can play them in the convenience of your own home or on your local practice putting green.

The bad news: There is no bad news. If you don't play them, your putting will continue as before, no harm done.

If you enjoy golf, competition, and self-improvement, and you want to improve your putting . . . you're really on to something here!

1.1

Not *Why*, Just *What* to Do

Dave Pelz's Putting Games Is Not a Book About "Why"

It's not about why you should hold your putter this way or that, or why you need a long or short shaft in your putter. I've already written about my research, testing, and opinions on putting in *Dave Pelz's Putting Bible*. If you want to get technical about the "whys" in your putting, read that book.

In these pages I explain and show what I believe to be the best and most efficient way to improve your putting. And I have a reason for writing this book now: my newly discovered "Easy-Access™" approach to learning, which I explain in the next two sections below.

1.2

Playing Games Has Proven Effective

You May Already Know, But In Case You Don't . . .

I've been researching and teaching the short game and putting for more than thirty years. I work with a staff of the finest short game and putting instructors, teaching two- and three-day Dave Pelz Scoring Game Schools in six locations across the United States (see www .pelzgolf.com for details) and one international location. We also teach one-day clinics in more than thirty cities around the United States each year. In addition, I have personally coached more than one hundred PGA and some eighty LPGA Tour Professionals over the last thirty years. I mention this because I want you to understand that the measurements and games described here have all been used and vetted in my schools and in my personal teaching. They work.

These games are not just based on ideas or theories. They've been used and proven effective. When golfers play them, their putting skills improve and they putt better on the golf course. So while the games themselves are not new, they are proven. What is new, and the reason I'm talking about easy access to learning in this book, are the learning aids that we've recently developed to go with the games.

1.3
"Easy-Access™" Is the New Game in Town

You Probably Have to Work for a Living

Most of us do. With work being a given, it's often difficult to spend enough time practicing *any* part of your golf game after work during the week to see improvement. On weekdays most golfers don't have the time or energy left in the evening to leave home, drive to a golf course, get all their clubs and balls onto the practice tee or green, and then practice. Even if you have the energy, the drive time alone (not to mention leaving the family) makes practicing after work prohibitive for most people.

To make this problem worse, it also requires time to take putting lessons from a pro. The practical reality is simple: Most golfers don't have time after work to drive back and forth from a golf course, take lessons from the pro, and then practice on the putting green. To do all of this often enough to make a difference simply does not fit into most golfers' lifestyles. And this doesn't even address the issue of the expense it takes to consistently mount such an effort to improve your putting.

But There's a New Game in Town

Would you like to play a few putting games at home in the evenings this week, without driving anywhere, and have that practice time improve your putting next weekend on the course? Would you be willing to spend fifteen to thirty minutes of fun time playing these games three nights this week (maybe with the kids), in exchange for holing four more putts next weekend? If your answer is yes to either of these two questions, read on!

The ability to make good putting strokes and to roll balls in the right direction at the proper speed is a simple motion. Good putters do it all the time. They make it look easy, because it is easy. However, the ability to consistently putt well eludes most golfers. And the ability to improve their putting has proven elusive even to golfers who practice on their own (with occasional advice and help from their buddies). The old adage that says "just forget everything and relate to the target" doesn't work well for golfers who have bad strokes or can't aim their putters. It just keeps them putting badly.

The truth is that a good putting stroke is a very simple motion. It doesn't take strength, agility, speed, or brainpower to swing a putter six or seven inches in each direction and roll a ball down a line. We all have enough strength, power, and brains to do this. And it doesn't take a genius to learn how far a good stroke will roll a ball. Again, we can all do it!

The Problem . . .

Most golfers never receive feedback on why their strokes are good or bad; they never understand why they make or miss putts; and they never learn to feel the difference between good and bad strokes. Hence, they've never known what to change, or how to improve. So when they've practiced and changed something, they've putted worse as often as they've putted better.

Without feedback, it's hard to learn even simple things well. Most golfers try to improve their putting with occasional practice, without professional instruction, on practice putting greens of unknown slope and speed, over footprints, spike marks, pitch marks, and grass imperfections, with occasional breezes blowing, and without *ever* knowing what they're doing right or wrong in their strokes. They simply practice putting and hope that by changing something, they'll become a better putter.

This is an almost impossible situation in which to improve—it's a terrible learning environment! But it's what most golfers have. And it keeps them in a state of "mild putting confusion" for their entire golf careers.

This Is Where This Book Comes In

Since putting is the easiest motion to make in golf, learning to do it properly is really quite achievable if you know *how* to learn it *and* receive good feedback during the process. Chapters 2, 3, and 4 detail the putting games you need to play, both on putting greens and at home, along with the feedback they provide. For those games you play at home, I explain how to utilize learning aids to receive better feedback. And the best part of all of this is the ease and convenience! Playing putting games at home is not only fun, it also doesn't take much time. You can do it in the evenings after work.

It's a great concept: Forget about driving anywhere—spend the few minutes and energy you have left at home in the evening playing putting games, having fun, and learning without even thinking about it. And it *will* improve your putting!

Some of the learning aids that make this possible (Touch Tutor™, AimLine Tutor™, Stroke Boot™, Face Boot™®) are small, easy-to-use, micro-electronic-memory systems (MEMS)–based devices that you putt on or attach to your putter. Other mechanical learning aids (Putting Track®, Teacher Clips™, Truthboard™, Putting Tutor™®) are used in our Dave Pelz Scoring Game Schools for putting. All measure and monitor your putting performance as you practice and play, to help you learn and improve more efficiently. They allow you to get great feedback by putting on carpets or SYN-Lawn® putting green surfaces at home in your family room, hallway, den, garage, or outdoors on your deck or backyard putting green. No hassle, no wasted time driving *anywhere* in the evening.

It is this concept of easy access to playing games and receiving the feedback necessary for learning—and getting both on a regular and consistent basis during the week *while you are at home*—that creates an environment for improvement in which you can better your putting skills as never before.

It's Almost "Game" Time

By scoring your game performances, practice turns into game time, competition, and fun. The competition can be played between you and a buddy, your kids, your spouse, or your own previous scores. It's a new improvement paradigm. Forget about driving to the course after work. Spend weekday evenings at home playing games and having fun. Then putt better on the course during the weekends.

1.4
Improving Is a Process

One thing I've learned from the thousands of putting lessons I've given is that golfers are more successful and learn more efficiently when they have a clear mental image and true understanding of two things: (1) exactly what they're going to try to accomplish, and (2) what they have to do to achieve it. That is, they need to know what their goals are, and how to practice to get to those goals.

I can't tell you how many golfers have said to me, "Dave, please tell me what to do. I can do almost anything I set my mind to, but I've never known how or what to practice to improve. Just tell me what to do, and I'll do it."

If this is your situation, you are one among many. Most golfers are willing to work to reach their goal *if* they know what they need to do to accomplish it. And when there's the added bonus of their work also being fun, then they've hit a home run! It's this process of first learning what you need to improve and then playing the right games to improve your weakness that has guided the organization of this book. You'll initially learn how to measure your putting strengths and weaknesses, then understand the purpose of each game, and finally how to play and keep score in the games (all games are similar in format and organization).

Putting Games Improvement Program

- Performance Games (to measure and evaluate your putting): Chapter 2
- Stroke Mechanics Games (to improve stroke skills): Chapter 3
- Touch and Feel Skill Games (to improve your mental skills): Chapter 4

As you read this, you're already well into the first step of our program, which is to organize your thoughts about putting in general and your own putting in particular before you start to play games. You need to understand and believe that improving your putting is achievable so that you'll commit to spending enough time playing games (three nights a week is minimum) to make a difference.

Learn How to Evaluate Your Putting Game in Chapter 2

You'll see how to measure your relative putting performance capabilities. This is not rocket science, but rather a loose application of the "scientific method" to find out which areas of your putting are weak or strong. You'll test your putting in seven areas: really short 3-foot putts, short 6-foot putts, makeable putts (10 to 20 feet), breaking putts (at least 6 inches of break), intermediate putts (20 to 30 feet), long lag putts (35 feet and longer), and three-putt avoidance. Once you find out where your putting is weak, it puts you in a perfect position to play the right games to optimize your improvement.

S olving the wrong problem won't fix the real problem. A guiding principle of our program is to improve the worst part of your putting first. Spending all of your time on what's right with your putting won't help you fix what's wrong with it. If you can't lag a long putt to stop within 6 feet of the hole, it won't help to work night and day on your short putts from 3 feet and in.

Before you can improve your weakest skill, you've got to know what it is. Maximum improvement in your putting will only be achieved by improving the weaknesses causing your putting problems. You'll not only enjoy measuring and recording your relative strengths/weaknesses, but also seeing a clear comparison of how you perform in every part of the putting game.

As in all of our two- and three-day Scoring Game Schools, the first step is to analyze your overall putting prowess. By measuring your relative performance levels in seven games, each measuring a different area of your putting, you can evaluate your scores in your own Putting Performance Chart (see a typical golfer's chart in Figure 1.4-1).

PUTTING PERFORMANCE CHART

3' Putt Circle (misses)	6' Putt Circle (misses)	Makeable Putts (score)	Breaking Putts (score)	Intermediate Putts (score)	Lag Putts (score)	Lag Putts (remainder)	3-Putt Avoidance (# Putts)
- 12 -							- 60 -
						- 1000 -	
- 11 -	- 12 -				- 60 -		
						- 900 -	
- 10 -	- 11 -	- 60 -					- 50 -
						- 800 -	
- 9 -	- 10 -		- 60 -	- 60 -	- 50 -		
	- 9 -	- 50 -				- 700 -	
- 8 -							- 40 -
	- 8 -		- 50 -	- 50 -			
- 7 -					- 40 -	- 600 -	
	- 7 -	- 40 -					
- 6 -			- 40 -	- 40 -		- 500 -	- 30 -
	- 6 -						
- 5 -					- 30 -	- 400 -	
	- 5 -	- 30 -					
- 4 -			- 30 -	- 30 -		- 300 -	- 20 -
	- 4 -						
- 3 -					- 20 -		
	- 3 -	- 20 -				- 200 -	
- 2 -			- 20 -	- 20 -			
	- 2 -					- 100 -	
- 1 -						- 50 -	
	- 1 -						
- 0 -	- 0 -	- 12 -	- 12 -	- 12 -	- 12 -	- 0 -	- 12 -

Figure 1.4-1

P lease understand that no matter how well or poorly you putt overall, you'll find that some of your putting performances (maybe your short putting or your lag putting) are clearly better or worse than others. I have never found any golfer whose putting performances were all the same (all good or all poor). Most golfers have one or two areas that pull down their overall putting results. You need to know if this is true for you, so you can identify the culprits and then "dial-in" to improve them.

Learn How to Play the Games in Chapters 3 and 4

Now we get to the heart of the learning process, which also happens to be the fun part: playing games to improve your stroke mechanics, touch, and feel. We consider where you aim your putter, what path you swing it on, where your putterface is aimed as it passes through impact, and where you contact your putts on your putterface as the physical fundamentals of your putting stroke. We classify the games you play to improve those aspects of your putting as games of "Stroke Mechanics," and they are detailed in Chapter 3.

The games you'll play to improve your putting touch, feel, and rhythm, or your ability to create and repeat meaningful preview strokes, are all classified as games of "Touch and Feel." These games that deal with your "mind's eye" are detailed in Chapter 4.

A Few Asides in Chapter 5 . . .

A quick read, Chapter 5 will clear up a few points that need to be understood if you're going to have a clear path to committing to this program. Once you finish Chapter 5, you'll be ready to begin your actual improvement process.

Do It in Chapter 6!

Start by playing the putting games that analyze your putting skills, and then switch to playing the games that will improve your weakest ones. I encourage you to keep these games light, relaxed, and open to anyone who wants to join you. The benefits are both enhanced and transferred to the golf course more effectively when you play in a competitive mode. This means either playing regularly with a competitor, or at least against your previous best scores (assuming you've kept track of those scores).

Competition Helps

The absolute best thing you can do is to compete in these games with someone who putts better than you do. The better they putt, the more focused and intense your own putting performance will have to be to compete. And the better that will be for your future putting. It may cost you a few bets here and there, but it's worth it. The quickest, most efficient way to get yourself focused during games is to need to bear down to keep from getting your butt kicked.

The reason that competition in games at home helps your on-course putting is that most golfers try really hard to perform well on the golf course. If you also try really hard to compete in games at home, you're practicing exactly like you're going to play, so when you improve in one you'll also improve in the other. Play smart: (1) be honest in your game scoring; (2) make your practice strokes and pre-putt ritual exactly as you make them on the golf course; and (3) play against the best competition you can find.

Recycle Your Skills Testing and
Take It to the Course

When you get to the end of Chapter 6, you've reached the final step of our program, which is to recycle. Retest yourself in the seven performance games and begin keeping track of your improvement (at least once a month is recommended, and never more than two months between tests). To keep learning and improving, you always need to be working on improving your weakest area. And if you spend a month practicing and playing games that target that one weakness, it may (or even probably will) no longer rank as the worst of your skills!

Work on Weaknesses, Then Play

Don't get stuck in a rut playing games you're really great at while ignoring the games that give you problems. And remember that you also need to get out on the course and play. Practice alone is never enough. It's the same with only playing and never practicing—neither is enough without the other.

1.5
A Few Facts to Consider

There are a number of facts, truths of the game, and statistics you should be aware of before embarking on a serious program to improve your putting. These items aren't earthshaking, but just re-member to keep the realities of putting somewhere in the back of your mind. Read these at least once. For those of you who understand and believe them already, just move on. If there are any items you don't understand or believe, please rethink them, because I'm con-vinced that they're true. And if you get stuck on any that bother you, do some more reading (in my *Putting Bible*) or talk to your local golf professional. It will help for you to have a clear mind to maximize the benefits that you'll receive from this game-playing program.

You need to know that . . .

- The starting line (direction) of your putts is primarily (83 percent) determined by the *angle* of your putterface at the moment of ball impact, while the *path* of your putter (assuming solid impact) has much less effect (17 percent) on its line.
- When most golfers work on getting their putts to start on-line, they focus on their putter path. But since they're working on only 17 percent of the problem (see statistic above), is it any wonder that most don't see any improvement after their practice?
- More putts from inside 20 feet are missed because of poor speed than because of poor starting line.
- For learning efficiently, bad feedback is worse than no feedback. So practice and play games carefully and score honestly.
- On any given slope, a putt's rolling speed affects how much it breaks (its line) on its way to the hole, so green speed is important to your putt's behavior.
- Not all putting games are of equal importance to all golfers. Golfers' putting skills and weaknesses vary as much as their signatures.
- All things being equal, short putts (inside of 6 feet) constitute about 50 percent of all putting, so converting your fair share of short putts is crucial to your game.
- Amateurs three-putt way too often. Most golfers can improve more by eliminating three-putts than by holing more putts of any particular length.

CHAPTER 2

Putting Performance Falls into Seven Areas

The first step in our program is to play seven "Performance" games to measure your putting ability in seven areas. This evaluation is vital to pinpointing where you have the greatest room for putting improvement. And while playing and scoring these games may be interesting, it does involve some effort and careful measurements. Documenting your performance may not be as much fun as playing our "Skill" games. To measure your performance you have to keep track of your scores in all seven games. This involves writing down and evaluating all of your scores relative to one another. But it's important to understand your weaknesses, so just go ahead and get this job done.

Testing Takes One Hour

To get started you'll need your putter, a dozen balls, thirteen tees, a tablet, a pen, and your 7-iron or a tape measure. You're then ready to go to a practice putting green where you can have a nice, quiet, personal "measure-your-putting-performance-in-seven-games" session.

This should take about an hour to complete if you have a companion to help set up the performance games, measure your putting results, and tabulate your scores on paper (you must record each of your game scores for later analysis). You can do all of this by yourself, but it won't flow as smoothly or as quickly as it will when you have a helper. It takes about ninety minutes when playing and scoring all seven games by yourself.

Always putt for a few minutes before you start testing, to get a feel for your stroke and the speed of the green for the day. Putt a few long putts, a few short ones, and a few others all around (downhill and uphill). Now it's time to get to work.

In the next three chapters I explain the what, where, when, why, and how of many putting games. To make the games easier to understand and use, each description is organized in the same way, as shown in the Putting Game Description list to the right. Game scoring is often based on where your putt stops relative to the hole (as seen in the Optimum Putted Ball Speed Scoring Map of Figure 2.0-1, with a few exceptions that will be noted later). Once you've read and understand our concepts in Chapters 1 and 6, this will enable you to jump to any part of the book, to any game, for a quick refresher on its rules and scoring.

PUTTING GAME DESCRIPTION

- Overview: purpose of game
- Description: how to set up and play
- Rules and Scoring: without/with feedback options
- How to Compete: options

OPTIMUM PUTTED BALL SPEED SCORING MAP

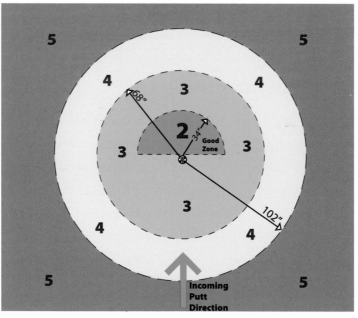

Figure 2.0-1

- Holed putts = 1
- Putts that stop in or touch the "good" zone = 2
- Putts that miss the good zone but stop within 68 inches of the hole = 3
- Putts that stop between 68 and 102 inches from hole = 4
- Putts that stop more than 102 inches from hole = 5
- Minimum possible score = 12; Par score = 24; Maximum possible score = 60

Twelve at a Time Is OK

Each of our seven performance games consists of only a twelve-putt sample. We use twelve putts to give us a snapshot of your putting ability in each area of putting. On any one day, it may not give you a 100 percent accurate picture of your overall putting capability, but don't worry about having a bad day and scoring low in one area. We all have bad days, and they balance out our better-than-average good days. Of course, a thousand samples in each game would result in a better evaluation, but testing twelve putts at a time is doable in a reasonable amount of time, and having twelve sample putts is way better than having none.

The good news is that measuring twelve putts per game several times over a period of a few months works really well. As the sample size mounts up, the uncertainty in the measurement of your performance goes down. In fact, by the time you've played three or four games in each putting category, you'll know for sure your relative ability to perform in all areas.

2.1
3-Foot-Circle Game

Overview

I first learned the *3-Foot-Circle Game* from Phil Mickelson, who got it from the great player and teacher Jackie Burke Jr. It's a great little game, and in this program we use it to measure the level of your performance in holing 3-foot putts. The 3-Foot-Circle Game is designed to:

1. Evaluate your ability to make 3-footers from all angles around the hole.
2. Help you learn to read putt break and green slope in the vicinity of the hole.
3. Teach you the best putt-speed vs. break-played trade-off for your short-putt results.

Yes, putts often break as they roll 3 feet to a hole. How much break you should "borrow" on such putts depends on what angle you putt from and how firmly you intend to roll the ball. The 3-Foot-Circle Game will teach you how to make this speed-vs.-break calculation for your own personal short putting.

Description

The 3-Foot-Circle Game is a test of twelve 3-foot putts, all rolled to the same hole. One putt is rolled from each of the twelve hourly positions of a clock, as though one were centered on the cup (see Figure 2.1-1).

Figure 2.1-1

Figure
2.1-4A

Figure
2.1-4B

of the fall line on the local slope. Watch each ball roll carefully from above and directly behind the hole until you find the downhill putt that does not break at all (Figure 2.1-4B).

Mark this "zero-break" location as the twelve o'clock putt position with your 7-iron grip when the 7-iron head is down in the hole (Figure 2.1-5).

Figure
2.1-5

Complete the setup by placing a sticker-dot (or tee) and ball at each of the other eleven clock-hour positions around the hole, with one exception being the six o'clock (straight uphill) putt position, which you should mark with two sticker-dots or tees (Figure 2.1-6).

Figure 2.1-6

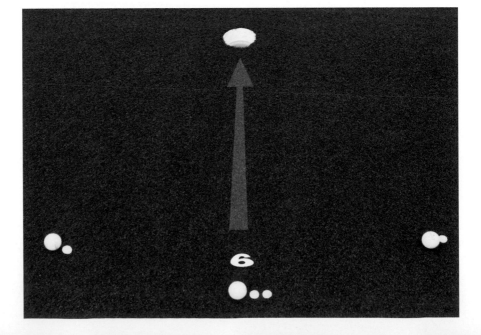

Rules and Scoring

Start by hitting the easiest putt, the dead-straight uphill putt from six o'clock. When putting this ball, the seven o'clock ball may interfere with your stance if you're putting right-handed (the five o'clock ball interferes with left-handers). In this case simply roll it aside until after putting from six o'clock, then replace it as you move forward in a counterclockwise motion, putting each hourly ball (five o'clock, four o'clock, three o'clock, and so on).

Scoring for the game is based on the number of putts you miss out of the total of twelve. (Note: Putt each ball only once; all putts after the first putt are given.) Every missed putt counts 1 point. The lower your score, the better you putted (minimum possible score = 0 if you make all twelve putts; maximum possible score = 12 if you miss them all).

How to Compete

Player No. 1 putts the six o'clock putt.

Player No. 2 putts the twelve o'clock putt (from the exact opposite side of the circle) for the first hole of competition. Missed putts count 1, made putts count 0.

For the next five holes, both players alternately putt from opposite sides of the circle in a match play format, both moving in a counterclockwise direction. (Note: Remove balls from the hole often enough to allow subsequent putts to fall cleanly into the hole.) After six holes, all balls must be replaced and the competition continues. Each competitor continues putting around the clock until he or she has rolled all twelve putts on the 3-foot circle.

The winner is the player with the lowest score in the 12-hole game (ties are played off at sudden death).

2.2
6-Foot-Circle Game

Overview

The *6-Foot-Circle Game* is exactly the same as the 3-Foot-Circle Game described earlier except that it involves 6-foot instead of 3-foot putts. The twelve clock-hour positions around the hole, the up- and down-hill orientation of the twelve o'clock to six o'clock direction along the fall line of the slope, and the scoring are all the same. The purpose of the game is to measure and score your ability to hole 6-footers.

You will notice immediately upon playing the game that 6-foot putts break significantly more than 3-footers (on the same slope of a green), and are therefore more sensitive to being rolled at or near the optimum putting speed. This characteristic becomes a major feature of the game when the hole is on a significant slope.

Description

Figure
2.2-1

The 6-Foot-Circle Game is a test of twelve putts, each rolled from one of the twelve hour positions of a clock around the cup (see Figure 2.2-1).

Just as in the 3-Foot-Circle Game, the line running between the clock positions of twelve and six o'clock is set to align precisely along the fall line of the slope around the hole. This means that when the green surface is perfect, putts should roll dead-straight up or down the hill from these two positions. The other ten putts will break varying amounts, with downhillers generally breaking more than uphillers.

Setup is accomplished by first rolling balls from above the hole until you find a downhill putt that rolls straight to the hole. Watch carefully from directly behind the roll until you find such a putt and then mark it as the twelve o'clock putt position. This time make sure all putts are 72 inches (about two 7-irons, Figure 2.2-2) from the hole.

Figure
2.2-2

Complete the setup by marking and placing a ball at each of the other eleven clock-hour positions around the hole, again with double tee (sticker-dot) markers at the six o'clock, straight-uphill position (Figure 2.2-3).

Figure 2.2-3

Rules and Scoring

Putt the easiest straight-uphill putt from six o'clock first.

Putt the next eleven balls while moving in a counterclockwise motion (for right-handers) from five o'clock, four o'clock, three o'clock, and so on, with the last putt being struck from the seven o'clock position. Putt each ball only once. Scoring for the game is the same as for the 3-Foot-Circle Game: Every missed putt counts as 1 point.

How to Compete

Player No. 1 rolls the six o'clock putt first.

Player No. 2 then rolls the twelve o'clock putt (from the exact opposite side of the circle) for his first putt.

For the next five holes, players alternately putt from opposite sides of the circle in a match play format (each player either makes or misses his first putt with each ball—no follow-up putts are allowed), moving around the clock in a counterclockwise direction. Balls must be removed from the hole often enough to allow putts to fall in without being affected or bounced out by a cup full of balls.

After six holes, all balls are replaced and the competition continues until both players have rolled all twelve putts around the 6-foot circle. The winner is the player who misses the fewest putts in the 12-hole game (ties are played off at sudden death).

2.3
Makeable-Putt Game

Overview

The intent of the *Makeable-Putt Game* is to measure your ability to hole putts in the seemingly very makeable 10- to 20-foot range, while also measuring how consistently you give these putts a chance to go in (by rolling them at or near the optimum putting speed).

Of course, no one ever makes all of their putts of this length, but the world's best putters convert somewhere between 20 and 33 percent of them, decreasing to about 10 percent as distance increases out to 20 feet (on excellent putting surfaces).

Some amateurs consistently hole a high percentage of putts in this distance range, but many golfers (including the occasional PGA and LPGA Tour player) seem to almost never make these putts! It's very interesting that the putting performance of golfers in the make-able-putt range is highly variable. The question is, where on the spectrum of conversion percentage does your makeable-putt perfor-mance lie?

Figure 2.3-1

Description

The Makeable-Putt Game consists of twelve putts, six each from two different directions and three different distances. Each cycle of six putts from one direction is composed of two putts from 15 feet, two putts from 20 feet, and two putts from 10 feet (see Figure 2.3-1).

To set up the game, first choose a hole you can putt to from two different directions, and walk three large steps straight away from the hole in one direction. Stick a tee (or a sticker-dot marker) in the green about a foot past the toe of your farthest foot (Figure 2.3-2) to mark a 10-foot distance from the cup.

Figure 2.3-2

Mark a 15-foot putt by taking one step sideways in a counter-clockwise direction, then two more big steps away from the hole. Place the marker behind your farthest foot (Figure 2.3-3).

Figure 2.3-3

Then finally take another step sideways and walk another two steps away from the hole and stick the third mark in or on the green behind your farthest foot, this one being about 20 feet from the hole (sideways steps stagger putting lines, so you won't roll longer putts over footprints made while putting shorter ones).

Next mark the green at the same three distances in the opposite direction from the hole. As you set up on future days, walk in different directions from whatever hole you choose so you'll also test your performance for up-, down-, and sidehill putts.

Putt two balls from each of the three distances as marked in one direction from the hole. Putt each ball only once.

Repeat the same cycle putting from the second (opposite, if possible) direction.

- Try to give yourself the best chance to hole every putt by rolling them at optimum putting speed (fast enough to help each putt hold its line and hit the hole, but slow enough to minimize lip-outs and overly long second putts).
- There's a 34-inch radius semicircular "good" zone behind the cup for makeable putts. The good zone is measured from the back edge of the hole and is square to the track of incoming putts, as measured to the end of a 7-iron grip with its head placed down in the hole (Figure 2.3-4).

Figure 2.3-4

- The measure of a putt successfully rolled at or near optimum speed is that it stops in the "good" zone behind the hole (if it does not go in). Putts hit with close-to-perfect speed will stop near the perfect center of the good zone, 17 inches past the hole.

A putt's score depends on where it stops relative to the Optimum Putted Ball-Speed Scoring Map (Figure 2.3-5), as shown below.

OPTIMUM PUTTED BALL SPEED SCORING MAP

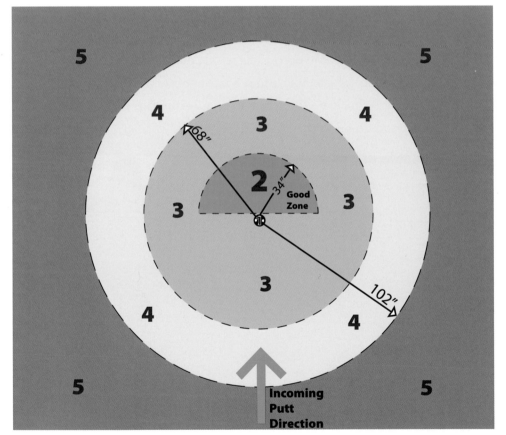

Figure
2.3-5

- Holed putts = 1
- Putts that stop in or touch the "good" zone = 2
- Putts that miss the good zone but stop within 68 inches of the hole = 3

- Putts that stop between 68 and 102 inches from hole = 4
- Putts that stop more than 102 inches from hole = 5
- Minimum possible score = 12; Par score = 24; Maximum possible score = 60

Your game score is the total of your twelve putt scores (the lower your score, the better your performance).

How to Compete

Both players alternate putting to the same hole from the same distance, but from opposite directions.

With two players, the Makeable-Putt Game becomes a match play competition. Whichever player scores lower on the first putt will be 1-up and putt first on the second putt. If both score the same, then the match is even going to the second putt.

After the first six putts, the players change directions to roll the last six putts of the game.

The game winner is the player who wins the most holes out of twelve (ties are played off at sudden death).

2.4
Breaking-Putt Game

Overview

The *Breaking-Putt Game* measures the quality of your putting performance for significantly breaking putts, where your ability to roll the ball at the proper speed is critical. Putts must break at least 6 inches down from their starting line direction as they roll to the hole from three makeable-putt distances (of 20 feet, 15 feet, and 10 feet).

The goal of the Breaking-Putt Game is to measure your ability to match the speed of a breaking putt to the line you have chosen to start it on, while maintaining near optimum rolling speed at the hole and avoiding three-putting the ones that miss.

Description

Each Breaking-Putt Game consists of twelve breaking putts in the makeable distance range of 10 to 20 feet. The more a putt breaks on its way to the hole, the more its line depends on the speed at which it rolls. Therefore, you need to find a hole in a green with enough slope to cause at least a 6-inch break in a putt from 15 feet. Makeable putts that break between 6 and 10 inches are common on most golf courses and putting greens.

The Breaking-Putt Game can be played for putts breaking up to 36 inches, but the more putts break, the more difficult they become. Don't go overboard and make things too difficult for yourself

It is well known that a breaking putt can be made when started on a "high" line if it's stroked with a deft touch to allow the ball to float softly down and into the hole, but the same putt can also be holed if it's rolled aggressively on a much lower line. An aggressively putted ball rolls with greater speed, breaks less, and holds a tighter line than a ball that's floated to the hole. Neither of these two techniques is right or wrong, but they're certainly different.

Figure 2.4-1   the first time you play. To set up for the game, walk around the putting green and find a hole in a smooth, significantly sloped area that has enough space to putt to the cup from both sides. Casually roll several 15-footers to this hole from different directions until you find one that breaks between 6 and 10 inches. Next walk off and mark your putting spots at 10 feet, 15 feet, and 20 feet on both sides from the cup (so that you'll be rolling both left-to-right and right-to-left breaking putts, Figure 2.4-1).

Rules and Scoring

- Try to give yourself the best chance to hole every putt by rolling the ball at optimum putting speed.
- All putts after each first putt are given.
- There's a 34-inch radius, semicircular "good" zone behind the cup for breaking putts. The good zone is measured from the back edge of the hole and is square to the track of incoming putts, as measured to the end of a 35-inch putter grip with its head placed down in the hole (Figure 2.4-2: Note that the ball on the left is in the good zone, while the ball on the right is out).

Figure 2.4-2

- A putt rolled at or near optimum speed will stop in the "good" zone behind the hole (if it doesn't go in). A putt hit at close-to-perfect speed will stop near the perfect center of the good zone, a point 17 inches past the hole.

Scoring for the Breaking-Putt Game is the same as for the Makeable-Putt Game (Figure 2.4-3):

OPTIMUM PUTTED BALL SPEED SCORING MAP

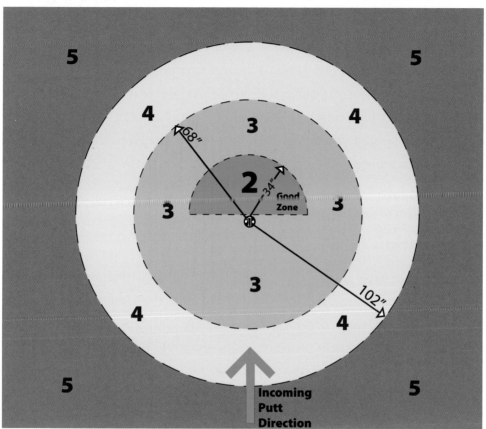

Figure 2.4-3

- Holed putts = 1
- Putts that stop in or touch the "good" zone = 2
- Putts that miss the good zone but stop within 68 inches of the hole = 3
- Putts that stop between 68 inches and 102 inches from hole = 4
- Putts that stop more than 102 inches from hole = 5
- Minimum possible score = 12; Par score = 24; Maximum possible score = 60

Your score for the game is the total of your twelve putt scores. The lower your score, the better your performance.

2.5
Intermediate-Putt Game

Overview

The *Intermediate-Putt Game* **measures** your putting performance in the 20- to 30-foot range. This is accomplished by measuring how well you control your roll distances to give putts a chance to go in, while minimizing your chance of three-putting. No one will ever make a high percentage of intermediate-length putts (due to green surface uncertainty, not through any fault of the golfer's own), but many golfers three-putt them on a regular basis.

Description

To accurately assess intermediate-length putting, the Intermediate-Putt Game uses the good zone behind the hole (the same zone used in the Makeable- and Breaking-Putt Games, as detailed in Chapters 2.3 and 2.4 earlier) to measure and score your speed control.

To set up the game you need to find a hole you can putt to from 30 feet away, in two different directions. Walk off and mark your putting spots by marking the green at 20, 25, and 30 feet in both directions from the cup (Figure 2.5-1A).

Figure 2.5-1A

Don't look for the most difficult downhill or breaking putts you can find for this test—the intent of this game is to measure your putting ability for the putts you normally encounter on the golf course.

Rules and Scoring

Start the Intermediate-Putt Game by putting two balls from 25 feet (Figure 2.5-1B), followed by two from 30 feet and two from 20 feet, all along the same direction from the hole.

Figure 2.5-1B

Then switch to the second group of markers in the second direction, and putt the same six-putt cycle again. As you play this game, remember: The focus of your mind's eye should be to roll each putt just past the hole. Not too far past, just a little (about a foot and a half) past so that each putt has a chance to go in but leaves you with little chance of missing the remaining putt.

Figure 2.5-2

The rules for the Intermediate-Putt Game are the same as for the Makeable-Putt Game above:

- Give yourself a chance to hole the putt by rolling the ball at the optimum putting speed. What's most important, however, is to not three-putt from this distance.
- A "good" zone (34-inch radius semicircular area) sits behind the hole for all intermediate-length putts. The front of the good zone is square to the track of incoming putts, and the back is easy to measure by using either a 7-iron or a 34- or 35-inch putter (Figure 2.5-2).

Scoring for the Intermediate-Putt Game is the same as for the Makeable-Putt Game (Figure 2.5-3):

- Holed putts = 1
- Putts that stop in or touch the "good" zone = 2
- Putts outside of the good zone, but within 68 inches of the hole = 3
- Putts that stop more than 68 inches but less than 102 inches from the hole = 4
- Putts that stop more than 102 inches from the cup = 5
- Minimum score = 12; Par score = 24; Maximum score = 60

OPTIMUM PUTTED BALL SPEED SCORING MAP

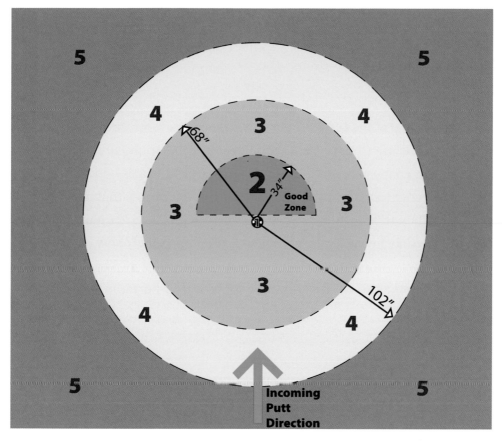

Figure
2.5-3

Your game score is your total for twelve putt scores: the lower, the better.

How to Compete

Both players putt to the same hole from different directions in match play.

Players alternate putting from each distance (in 25-foot, 30-foot, and then 20-foot putting order). Whichever player scores lower on the first putt wins the hole. If both scores are the same, the hole is tied.

After the first six putts, players change directions for the second six putts.

The winner is the player who wins the most of twelve holes (ties are played off in sudden death, match play format).

2.6
Lag-Putt Game

Overview

The goal of the *Lag-Putt Game* is to measure your ability to roll long putts close to the hole. Of course you'd like to make them, but that won't happen often because of the many challenges—including green speed, green surface quality, and green-reading—that are involved. Although it's really fun when you do happen to get lucky and hole one (like my lucky 210-footer on a Golf Channel show, Figure 2.6-1), it's way more important to control your speed and leave your long putts close to the hole, so that you can two-putt almost every time.

Figure 2.6-1

Description

The majority of poor lag-putts are poor because they're rolled the wrong distance. Most golfers roll them in pretty much the right direction, but controlling lag-putt distance is a real problem. Few golfers realize that they could lower their scores by improving their lag-putting performance, and they hardly ever practice this aspect of their putting.

If this game indicates that you have a lag-putt problem, you'd be well advised to start working on it immediately, because you'll face lag-putts in every round you play for the rest of your golf career.

The Lag-Putt Game consists of twelve total putts (in two six-putt cycles) from three different "reference" distances. The lag "reference" distances of 40 feet, 50 feet, and 60 feet are used both in my personal teaching and in our schools because they're so frequently encountered. Once golfers develop the skill to handle these three distances, they can finesse their putting touch to other distances and perform well on most long putts.

To set up, first choose a hole that supplies space along a direction that allows you to putt from all three reference distances. Walk this direction, counting thirteen large steps straight away from the hole. Place a sticker-dot in the green about one foot past the toe of your farthest foot (Figure 2.6-2) to mark a 40-foot distance back to the cup.

Figure 2.6-2

Figure 2.6-3A   From the 40-foot marker, take three more steps in the same direction and place another marker a foot past your farthest foot for a 50-foot putt. Finally, walk another three steps (plus a foot) for your 60-foot putt marker (see Phil Mickelson setups for this game at several major championships in Figures 2.6-3A and 2.6-3B).

Figure 2.6-3B

Don't bother with a reference putt at 100 feet because you don't encounter putts that long very often, and your performance from there doesn't affect your score much. Roll a few putts from 100 feet every once in a while just so you're not in shock when you eventually get a putt that long, but it's more important to be a good lag putter from 40, 50, and 60 feet than it is from any other distance. (Note: As you set up on future days, walk in different directions from the hole so you can test your performance on up-, down-, and sidehillers.)

Rules and Scoring

Putt two balls from each of the three reference distances in the following order: two from 50 feet, two from 60 feet, and two from 40 feet. You should change putt distances every two putts, always starting with the middle length first (Figure 2.6-3C).

Then go to the longest putt second, and back to the shortest putt third, so that your touch is challenged to adjust frequently. The better you perform this challenge in games, the better you'll be able to adjust your touch for the new distance you face on every putt on the golf course.

Figure 2.6-3C

After you've rolled the first six putts, repeat the same six-putt cycle in the same order.

- In the Lag-Putt Game you're tested on your ability to lag long putts close to the hole, preferably within 3 feet. There is no emphasis on holing long putts.
- There's a 34-inch radius, semicircular "good" zone behind the cup for lag putts. The good zone is measured either with a tape measure at 34 inches from any edge of the hole, or by the length of a 7-iron or a 35-inch putter shaft to the end of the grip, when the head is down in the hole (Figure 2.6-4).

Figure 2.6-4

- The measure of a successful lag putt is that it stops in or touches the good zone around the hole, or happens to luck into the hole.

There are two methods for scoring the Lag-Putt Game: A "Stroke" score based on the Lag-Putt Scoring Map (Figure 2.6-5), and a "Putt-Remainder" score based on how far each lag putt stops from the hole (measured in inches).

Scoring by "Stroke" method (see Figure 2.6-5):

LAG PUTTING SCORING MAP

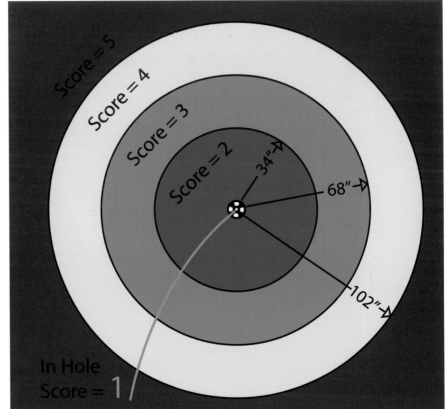

Figure 2.6-5

- Holed putts = 1
- Putts that come to rest in or touching the "good" zone (i.e., 34 inches) = 2
- Putts that stop outside good zone, but within 68 inches (two putter lengths) of the hole = 3

- Putts that stop between 68 and 102 inches (between two and three putter lengths) = 4
- Putts that stop more than 102 inches (three putter lengths) from the hole = 5
- Minimum possible score for twelve-putt game = 12; Par = 24; Maximum possible score = 60

Your "Stroke" score for the Lag-Putt Game is the sum total of your twelve putt scores.

Scoring by the "Putt-Remainder" method:

- A putt remainder is the distance from the point at which your putt comes to rest to the edge of the hole (Figure 2.6-6).
- Holed putts = zero remainder.
- Scoring by the Putt-Remainder method requires the most effort, but it's the most accurate way to measure lag performance.
- Game score by the Putt-Remainder method is the total of your twelve putt remainders.

Figure 2.6-6

How to Compete

Players alternately putt in the normal sequence of distances: first 50 feet, then 60 feet, then 40 feet.

Each player putts twice from each distance, then repeats cycle for twelve putts total.

The Lag-Putt Game competition is match play and can be played using either of the two scoring methods detailed above. It's important to choose your scoring method before the game starts. Whichever player scores lower on the first putt will be 1-up, the other 1-down. If both scores are the same (often true in "Stroke" scoring, but seldom true in "Remainder" scoring), the match is even going to the second putt.

The winner is the player who wins the most holes out of twelve (ties are played off in sudden death).

2.7
Three-Putt-Avoidance Game

Overview

The overall goal of the *Three-Putt-Avoidance Game* is to measure your ability to avoid three-putting when faced with long putts under more difficult than normal putting conditions. Such conditions might include having to face long putts on days when the wind is strong and gusting, or having to putt on greens that are extra bumpy or on severely sloping greens that have gotten out-of-control fast. In these conditions, avoiding a three-putt becomes very difficult, and we simulate this extra difficulty in the Three-Putt-Avoidance Game by making each putt (after the first putt) extra long. The fact is that golfers three-putt more often than the quality of their putting strokes deserves, because on some days the "golf gods" are extra critical when it comes to lag-putting. They throw a grain direction into how the grass grows on some greens but not on others, and they move the wind around to unexpectedly affect the roll of long putts. This may not sound fair to you, but get over it: It's the game we all love to play, and you need to deal with it.

Description

To avoid three-putting long putts, golfers need to: (1) have their "touch" on high alert, (2) carefully observe the last 5 feet of their first putt's roll to see how it breaks, and (3) stay positive and focused when the winds of the golf gods unexpectedly give them a second putt that is longer than they deserve.

This is important, because three-putts often do more than waste one stroke: They can demoralize and anger a golfer, and often trigger disasters on subsequent holes. Every golfer knows they have enough strength, talent, coordination, and brains to be capable of two-putting most of the time. So why are there so many three-putts?

IS LAG-PUTTING FAIR?

On short putts, when you read the green well and execute a good stroke, you see a good roll and usually make the putt. The same truth extends out to makeable- and even intermediate-putt lengths, but with less and less frequency. This is fair and reasonable: The longer the putt, the less likely you are to make it. So as putts get longer than 35 feet, we should make fewer of them, and maybe begin to see a few three-putts.

But that's not what happens. All of a sudden, when putt lengths exceed 30 feet, golfers seem to three-putt exponentially more often because:

1. Long putts roll on imperfect greens for long periods of time; the longer they roll, the more susceptible they are to gusting winds.
2. Due to emotional responses, golfers look away from long putts and thus don't see how their ball breaks around the hole. This decreases the probability of holing the second putt.
3. Even if you put a good stroke on a lag-putt, your ball may—or may not—end up close to the hole.

So you've got to be on super-high alert to roll a really good first putt, because it may get a little something added to or taken away from its roll that you didn't really deserve. And you've also got to watch carefully as your lag-putt rolls to a stop. The ball's final 5 feet of roll will show the slope of the green around the hole.

To handle these conditions, the Three-Putt-Avoidance Game makes lag putting tougher than you deserve and more difficult than is fair. It adds 34 inches to the length of each second (and following missed) putt, to see how you handle unfair events on the greens. The game consists of twelve total putts (in two six-putt cycles) from the three different lag "reference" distances (40 feet, 50 feet, and 60 feet, just like the Lag-Putt Game), except that 34 inches is added to every putt length (after the first putt), before you attempt to putt out.

To set up a Three-Putt-Avoidance Game, first choose a hole that supplies space for you to putt from all three of the lag reference distances, and mark those distances.

Figure
2.7-1

Rules and Scoring

Putt two balls from each of the three reference distances in the following order: two from 50 feet, two from 60 feet, and two from 40 feet.

After the first two 50-foot putts come to rest, draw each ball back 34 inches straight away from the hole (Figure 2.7-1) and putt out both balls from their new positions.

Is this fair? No, but that's the game—try to two-putt them both anyway. When you miss a second putt, again add 34 inches before you try the third putt, and then try to hole it.

Continue this 34-inch penalty on all missed putts until each ball is holed (Figure 2.7-2 shows the second drawback required for a three-putt, with my svelte figure and putter ghosted in for the first 34-inch drawback).

Figure 2.7-2

After you've putted out twice from each of the three reference distances (after adding 34 inches to each putt required after the first), you're ready to repeat the same cycle once again from the same three distances, in the same order.

This game offers you twelve chances to avoid three-putting, with each remaining putt getting an extra 34-inch "spiff" of difficulty added, just to see how you handle it.

- After each (of twelve) first putts from three reference distances, add 34 inches to your second putts before attempting to hole them out.
- If any second putts are missed, add the same 34 inches of extra distance to each following putt before putting out.
- Your score for the game is the total number of putts taken to hole out from twelve initial lag putts. The lower your score, the better you've performed.
- Minimum possible score = 12 (if you holed every first lag putt, but this probably won't ever happen); Par = 24; Maximum possible score = very high, if played on undulating and fast greens (be aware—this is a difficult game).

How to Compete

Two players putt alternately from the same distance to the same hole, maintaining the normal sequence of putt distances (twice from 50 feet, 60 feet, and then 40 feet) in two cycles.

Each player draws his own ball back 34 inches from the point where each missed putt comes to rest, directly away from the hole, before putting out.

Competition is match play for twelve holes (ties are played off in sudden death).

WE'VE DESIGNED FOUR GAMES TO IMPROVE YOUR SKILLS IN executing stroke mechanics. Each game focuses on your ability to execute one of the four stroke fundamentals that have primary effects on your putting results: how well you aim your putter (*Aim Game*); what path your putter follows relative to your desired putt starting line (*Path Game*); how your putterface aligns to your initial putt line at the moment of impact (*Face-Angle Game*); and where on your putterface you make ball contact (*Impact Game*).

Each game is designed to provide feedback as to how well or how poorly you're performing the skill in question. When available, multiple options for providing the feedback necessary for efficient learning are described. The games are easy to set up, fun to play, and the more you play them . . . the better you'll putt.

3.1
Aim Game

Overview

The better golfers aim, the better they putt. It's a measurable fact. If and when you improve your aim, the in-stroke corrections necessary to start putts on-line are decreased, and your putting will improve.

The goal of playing the Aim Game is to train and improve your ability to aim your putter consistently and accurately along the line on which you want your putts to start on short and makeable-length putts. We don't recommend spending significant time practicing aim for the intermediate and lag-putt distances, because you can't read the break on these longer putts well enough to know precisely where to aim anyway.

Description

It's important to internalize the knowledge that:

1. Good aim is fundamental to good putting;
2. The better you aim, the better you'll putt;
3. Bad aim requires bad in-stroke compensations; and
4. The shorter the putt, the more important the aim.

Aim is critically important for short putts. Your stroke on these putts is short, and if you aim poorly, there's precious little time or room to compensate for that error. Poor aim on makeable-length putts poses a different problem. While there is more time to compensate for poor aim within your stroke, these compensations make your stroke more complex and less repeatable.

We consider improving aim a part of improving putting stroke mechanics, because aim accuracy determines how much error your stroke mechanics must compensate for to start putts on-line.

Each Aim Game evaluates the accuracy of your putter's actual aim just before your stroke takeaway (relative to perfect alignment) for twelve putts by measuring the alignment to each of three distances along your putting line. To set up, first choose a putting spot that allows you to aim at three different target distances and place a sticker-dot there. Then place three "Phony Hole" targets (or soda bottles or cans) at the three distances of 10, 15, and 5 feet (Figure 3.1-1).

If your room is not large enough to accommodate the longer target distance, it's okay to bring it in a little, but keep the short putt distances at 5 feet and 10 feet.

Figure 3.1-1

For your final setup, place a book as a blocking plate in front of your putting spot, so your putts won't hit and move your targets (Figure 3.1-2).

Figure 3.1-2

Then get your putter, twelve balls, and any learning aid you want to use, and you're ready to putt.

The putting sequence for the Aim Game proceeds as listed below.

Putting Sequence for a Twelve-Putt Aim Game

- First two putts: at 10-foot target.
- Second two putts: at 15-foot target
- Third two putts: at 5-foot target
- Above cycle of six putts is repeated

The final alignment of your putterface immediately before you start the backswing of your stroke is the aim that is measured and scored. For every putt, you receive an aim score based on the way you measure (see scoring details below). Your total Aim Game score is the average of your twelve individual aim scores.

Rules and Scoring

THE AIM GAME PLAYED WITH A *TEACHER® POINTER*

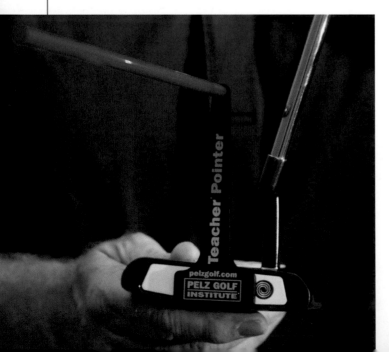

The Aim Game can be played using a "Teacher Pointer" (Figure 3.1-3), putting in the distance sequence as described above (i.e., two putts at each of three distances, cycle of six putts repeated a second time).

The Teacher Pointer positions a large red straw so that it points perpendicularly out from the putterface. The straw points in the direction the putterface is aimed,

Figure 3.1-3

which can be seen and measured within reasonable accuracy by a second person standing directly behind you (with a small piece of string) as you aim and roll putts.

The accuracy of your alignment measurements will depend on the attention and accuracy of your second helper person, and is measured against a scale of a paper/cardboard strip marked in inches at the shortest distance target (Figure 3.1-4).

These markings provide a metric for measuring aim, covering

Figure 3.1-4

one foot out to the right (+) and left (-) of the target. Your scoring partner observes your pointer straw alignment and, when you "think" you're aiming directly at each of your targets, records where you're actually aiming (just before each of your twelve putts).

It's easy for your partner to measure alignment by holding a string that's aligned between the ball and your target in front of one eye (with the other eye closed) and using this as a reference to perfect alignment. They should then simply move the top end of the string (keeping the bottom end over the ball) to point where your putter pointer is aiming just before you putt, and read how far right or left the string crosses the cardboard metric on either side of the short target.

Score for the Aim Game is measured in inches to the right or left of the 5-foot distance target, even when you are aiming and stroking putts to longer targets (the angular error is the same). Individual putt-aim error scores can range from zero up to some very high numbers for very bad aimers. I've never seen a perfect (zero) average game score.

PLAYED WITH A *LAZRAIMER*®

LazrAimers® have been used in our schools to help students improve their putter aim for many years. The device operates by voice activation, turning on a laser beam that shoots out and bounces off your putterface mirror and back toward the target. With a LazrAimer (Figure 3.1-5), you play the Aim Game by making your preview stroke first, then putting two putts to each of three targets at 5 feet, 10 feet, and 15 feet, all lined up in the same direction, and then repeating the cycle for a total of twelve putts.

Figure 3.1-5

During final setup before each putt (after you've achieved the final aim of your putter and are looking down at the ball, but before you start the backswing of your stroke), you say the word "on." This command turns on the laser beam, which bounces off your putterface mirror and shows up as a bright red spot on the wall behind the target. Although you don't look up, the red spot indicates a relative aim-error of your putterface (above your target because of putterface loft) to the right or left of your target. Your scoring helper moves his string to read your aim error score (the same as for the Teacher Pointer described above) in inches right or left of the 5-foot target.

The setup and playing of the Aim Game using a Face Boot in its Aim (A) mode (Figures 3.1-6A and 3.1-6B) . . .

Figure 3.1-6A

Figure 3.1-6B

. . . is the same as described earlier for the LazrAimer, except you don't need the paper/cardboard inch markers to the left and right of the targets, or another person to take your aim measurements. The Face Boot measures alignment for you.

The Aim Game putting sequence and three distances are the same as for the LazrAimer described above. With the Face Boot, however, before you address putts at each new distance, you must repeatedly identify "perfect aim" to the Boot by aligning your putter with the aim-plate positioned behind your ball (Figure 3.1-7).

Figure 3.1-7

Then, as you align your putter to the appropriate targets in the Aim Game, the Face Boot-A measures your putter alignment immediately before you stroke your putts.

Note: We make our own "sticker-dots" because we use so many of them. Any office supply store has similar Avery® dots available, or any small piece of tape will suffice. Aim-plates can be made using a T-square and cardboard. They are also supplied with the Face Boots, available at www.pelzgolf.com.

The Face Boot-A measures, scores, and reads out your aim accuracy in inches to the right or left of your target after every putt. After twelve putts, the twelve individual aim errors are averaged and displayed (blinking) for your game score.

How to Compete

Whether using Teacher Pointers, LazrAimers, or Face Boots (in the Aim mode), both players putt alternately along the same aim line to the same target distance.

Putting proceeds in the same sequence as normal for the Aim Game. As each player aims and putts, his or her competitor (or helper, or Face Boot-A) watches and scores the aim for that stroke.

Whichever player scores lower on the first putt will be 1-up, the other 1-down. If both scores are the same, the match is even going to the second putt.

The game is scored in match play. The winner is the player who wins the most holes out of twelve (ties are played off in sudden death). Note: To compete with Face Boots, each player must have his own, attached to his own putter.

3.2
Path Game

Overview

The intent of the *Path Game* is to train and improve your ability to swing the putter in a consistently repeatable and effective path through the impact zone of your stroke. There are two stroke paths consistent with good putting: (1) a pure-in-line-square stroke (PILS), also known as a straight-back-straight-through (SBST) stroke along the intended starting line of your putt, and (2) an Arc or curved stroke motion tangent to the putt start line and curving (arcing) slightly around your body on both sides of the putt-line tangent point (Figures 3.2-1A and 3.2-1B).

Figure 3.2-1A

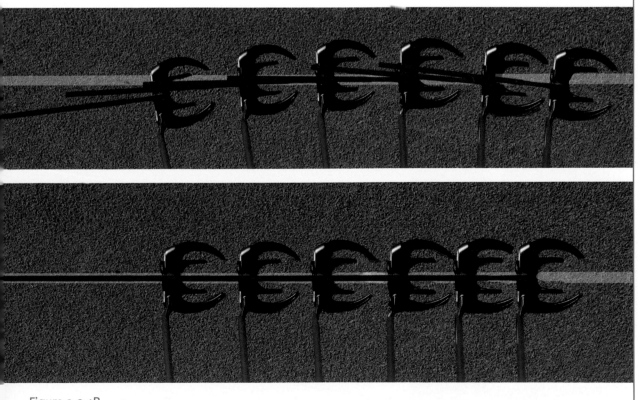

Figure 3.2-1B

Even though errors in your putter's path through the impact zone are only transferred to your putt's starting line with 17 percent efficiency, it is still always good for your putting results if you can improve the consistency and repeatability of your stroke path.

Description

The Path Game is designed to help you learn the feel of your stroke (it's your choice of PILS or Arc, but don't try learning both) and commit it to habit (groove it) so that it'll stand up under pressure. Each game gives you a path evaluation score for each stroke in a series of twelve—relative to the perfect putting stroke. You'll also have an average game score for all twelve strokes combined.

The game is played by putting two balls to each of three distances (10 feet, 15 feet, and 5 feet) in sequence, followed by a repeat of the same six-putt cycle. This twelve-putt game can be repeated over and over again to improve your ability to swing your putter in a more consistent and repeat-able stroke-path motion.

There are two learning aids used to play path games: a *Putting Track* and a *Stroke Boot-P* (in Path mode).

Rules and Scoring

If you use the Putting Track (Figure 3.2-2) the track rails should be spaced apart using a separation bar, plus additional spacer washers if needed, to create the appropriate space (details in the sidebar below)

Figure 3.2-2

in one of the three tolerances, relative to the width of your putterhead (measured heel to toe, Figure 3.2-3).

Figure 3.2-3

Play your first Path Game with a "Pro" setting (¾ inch total spacing between putterhead and rails) and count your number of "poor" strokes. A poor stroke will produce a sound from your putterhead if it hits the track rail. If there is no sound for the entire stroke, you've made a "good" stroke.

SPACE SETTINGS OF THE PUTTING TRACK

Putterhead width plus 1 inch = Standard Tolerance

Putterhead width plus ¾ inch = Pro Tolerance

Putterhead width plus ½ inch = Super-Pro Tolerance

Adjust your skill tolerance setting of the track periodically thereafter, as dictated by these guidelines:

> **Good**: 0 to 3 Poor Strokes = Your track separation is too great for the quality of your stroke, and you should advance to the next higher (more difficult) setting for the next game.
>
> **OK**: 4 to 8 Poor Strokes = Your track spacing is optimized for your current stroke-path accuracy. Maintain the current setting for your next game.
>
> **Poor**: 9+ Poor Strokes = Your track separation is too tight for the quality of your stroke. Use the next lower (less difficult) setting for the next game.

The reason for these guidelines is to optimize learning efficiency during play. It's easier to feel the difference between poor and good strokes if you have about 50 percent of each during the game. Con-

the desired path line (too far away from the golfer). A low-pitched signal identifies a putter swinging inside the desired putter path (too close to the golfer). The louder the off-line signal from the Stroke Boot-P, the farther off-line the putter is from the perfect path. A zero signal (quiet) during the stroke means the putter is perfectly on-path.

After each putting stroke is completed, the Stroke Boot-P measures and scores how far, and for how long, the putter path swung inside or outside the desired putter path from the start of the backswing to the end of the follow-through. The score for each stroke is then displayed on the Stroke Boot's bottom LCD. After the twelfth stroke is completed and scored, the Stroke Boot-P will total and report (in Blinking mode) the average of all twelve of your stroke scores, which is your Path Game score.

How to Compete

Each of two players must have his or her own track set to their own difficulty tolerance (Standard, Pro, Super-Pro) and aimed for the stroke path they've chosen to groove (PILS vs. Arc).

Both players putt alternately to the same sequence of target distances (10 feet, 15 feet, and 5 feet, two putts to each), as in the normal Path Game (all balls should be rolled into pillows).

Scoring is based on whether or not the putters touch either track rail during the stroke. Competition is match play for twelve holes (ties are played off in sudden death).

To play competitively with the Stroke Boot-P, each player must have his or her own Stroke Boot set to the appropriate path (PILS or Arc) mode. Putts should be rolled alternately as in the normal Path Game (balls rolled into pillows). Scoring is based on stroke-path scores reported after each stroke by the Stroke Boot-P. Competition is match play for twelve holes (ties are decided by the lowest game score as winner).

3.3
Face-Angle Game

Overview

The face angle (or aim) of your putter at the exact moment of ball impact basically determines the line that your putts start on (Figure 3.3-1).

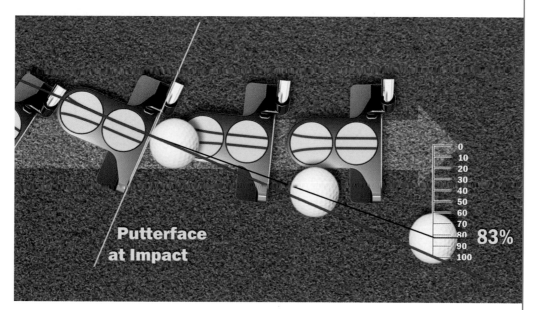

Figure 3.3-1

Once you choose your starting line and aim your putter, any alignment error that then creeps into your stroke at impact will cause putts to start off-line by 83 percent of that error (compared with 17 percent transfer efficiency from putter path error). Your putter must be substantially square to the intended line of your putts at impact in order to have any chance of starting putts on-line consistently.

To a significant degree, your ability to deliver a square strike (a square putterface) to your putts will dominate your success in starting putts rolling on-line and without sidespin. The "squareness" of your putter at impact is critical to your putting success!

Description

The Face-Angle Game measures and coaches you to improve your ability to start putts on-line in a series of twelve putts. It is played:

on a carpet with one of three feedback devices (detailed below) to three different distances;

in the sequence of two putts to each distance target (10 feet, 20 feet, and 5 feet) (Figure 3.3-2).

Figure 3.3-2

The six-putt sequence is then repeated for a twelve-putt game. In each game you receive a face-angle evaluation or score after each putt. Your game score is your total score for twelve putts.

Face-Angle games should be repeated several times each session (each game takes five to ten minutes), several times each week, until your performance improves substantially. Also keep track of your Face-Angle Game scores over time to document your progress, as you teach yourself to deliver a higher and higher percentage of square strikes to putts.

Treat each putt within a game as a new event. Make at least one practice (preview) swing looking at the target before each stroke, to "feel" the putt/stroke-length relationship, as you normally do on the golf course.

Rules and Scoring

PLAYING THE "FACE-ANGLE GAME" WITH A PUTTING TUTOR

You can set up a Putting Tutor (Figure 3.3-3) outdoors on a green or indoors on most carpets.

Figure 3.3-3

Place the Putting Tutor on the spot from which you're going to putt, with three appropriately placed targets at 10 feet, 20 feet, and 5 feet. Make sure the Tutor AimLine™ is properly oriented along the intended starting line of your putt, and place the two marbles (which form a gate) in the appropriate tolerance recesses (Figure 3.3-4).

Figure 3.3-4

Standard tolerance recesses (left in Figure 3.3-4) allow the largest margin of error for off-line putts. The Pro tolerance (center in photo) allows for less off-line error, while the most difficult (tightest) gate tolerance is the Super-Pro marble position (right in Figure 3.3-4 photo).

Start each game with twelve golf balls sitting beside your Putting Tutor. Putt one ball at a time toward your appropriate target distance. Every time a putt dislodges a marble it counts as a "poor" stroke. (If both marbles are dislodged by a putt, it still counts as one poor stroke.) The fewer poor strokes (out of twelve), the lower your score, and the squarer your putterface is through impact in your stroke.

Play your first Face-Angle Game using the "Pro" marble tolerance. Thereafter, if you consistently dislodge three or fewer marbles in twelve putts, you're ready to play the next game at the next-tighter marble tolerance. If you regularly dislodge nine or more marbles in twelve strokes, you should play with a looser tolerance position.

WITH AN AIMLINE TUTOR-FA

The *AimLine Tutor-FA* **(Face-Angle mode)** (Figure 3.3-5), is an electronic

Figure 3.3-5

version of the Putting Tutor described above. The setups for both are similar, except that no marbles are required with the AimLine Tutor-FA, it is used indoors on a carpet, and it keeps track of your stroke scores for you. The AimLine Tutor-FA evaluates (and reports) each stroke in two ways.

1. Putt Score (top LCD): Based on where the putt would have stopped relative to your target (on a 10-foot green-speed, perfectly flat surface), as determined by the Optimum Putted Ball Speed Scoring Map (Figure 3.3-6).

2. Putt Line Accuracy (lower LCD): How far off-line the putt would have rolled at the target distance (Figure 3.3-7).

OPTIMUM PUTTED BALL SPEED SCORING MAP

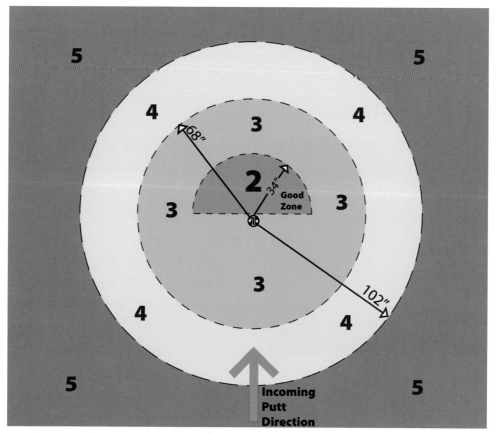

Figure 3.3-6

PUTT SCORE:

1. Putt rolled into hole.
2. Putt missed hole, but stopped in "good" zone within 34 inches past hole.

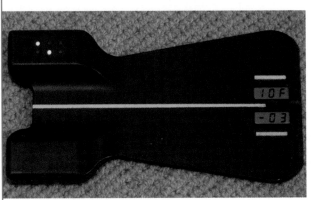

3. Putt missed good zone but stopped within 68 inches of hole.
4. Putt missed hole by between 68 and 102 inches.
5. Putt missed hole by more than 102 inches.
6. Putt Miss-Distance left (-) or right (+) of hole in inches (bottom LCD) at target distance (Figure 3.3-7).

Figure 3.3-7

After the results of the twelfth putt have been reported, the AimLine Tutor-FA flashes two blinking scores for your overall game performance (average putt score and average off-line error absolute value).

WITH A FACE BOOT-FA

Figure 3.3-8

The Face Boot (Figure 3.3-8) fits on the bottom of your putter and is a very different device from the two Tutors described above. Although you can use it to play the same Face Angle game, it measures a different part of your putting stroke and gives feedback in a totally different way. While the Putting Tutor and the AimLine Tutor both measure the accuracy with which your putts start on-line vs. off-line, the Face Boot measures and scores how close to square your putter stays (relative to your stroke path) as you swing back and forward during your stroke.

In its "Game" mode, the Face Boot-FA gives high- and low-pitched audible "squareness" feedback on your putterface in real time as you swing your putter. A high-pitched signal means the putterface is open (aimed to the right) relative to the desired putt line (for right-handers). A low-pitched signal identifies a putterface that's aimed to the left (closed). The louder either signal sounds, the farther off-square the putterface is. A zero signal during your stroke (dead quiet) is the sign of a "square" putterface. The device also gives you a "squareness" measurement on its bottom LCD panel after each stroke (Figure 3.3-9)

After the score for the twelfth putt has been reported, the LCD panel displays your average squareness score (flashing) for all twelve strokes, which is your game score.

The Face Boot-FA measures the squareness of your putterface relative to either of two stroke motion options: the "Pure-In-Line-Square" (PILS) stroke—straight back and through along your putt aim line—or the "Arc" motion, which curves around your body in a "screen-door" stroke

Figure 3.3-9

How to Compete

With a Putting Tutor on a carpet, players alternate putting to each of three distances—10 feet, 20 feet, and 5 feet—and then repeat the six-putt sequence a second time.

Both players putt through the same performance tolerance settings of the marbles (Standard, Pro, or Super-Pro). Putts should be rolled into a pillow.

Scoring is based on whether or not marbles are dislodged on

each putt. Ties may be carried over or not, to be mutually agreed on by the players. Competition is match play for twelve holes (ties are played off in sudden death).

With an AimLine Tutor-FA, two players alternate putting to each of the three distances as above. Putts are rolled into a pillow.

Scoring is at match play, based on the putt score for each putt. Ties may be carried over or not, to be mutually agreed upon by the players. Competition is match play for six holes (ties are played off in sudden death). Note: The twelve-putt average putt and off-line scores reported at the end of competitive games are not meaningful and cannot be used, because both players' scores and errors are totaled together in the averages.

With the Face Boot-FA, each player must have his or her own Face Boot set to the PILS or Arc stroke mode they use. Putts are rolled alternately to the same sequence of distances (10 feet, 20 feet, 5 feet, 10 feet, 20 feet, 5 feet), as used in the normal Face-Angle Game (balls putted into a pillow). Scoring is based on the squareness scores reported after each stroke.

Competition is match play for twelve holes (tie games are decided by the lowest average game score).

3.4
Impact Game

Overview

The intent of the *Impact Game* is to train and improve your ability to strike putts solidly on or near the sweet spot of your putterface. Solid impact is important in putting because it affects the distance your putts roll.

When you putt, your stroke controls how fast your putter swings and where you contact the ball on the putterface. This second factor, the location of impact on the putterface, controls the percentage of putterhead energy transferred to the ball. Both factors affect rolling speed and roll distance of your putts (Figure 3.4-1).

Figure 3.4-1

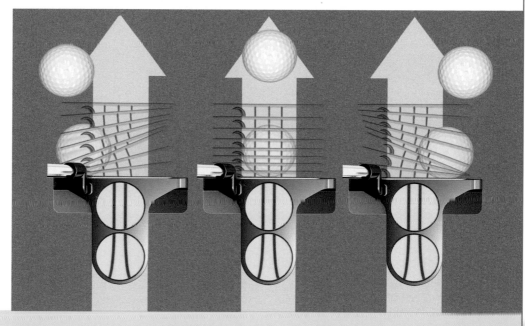

The closer you strike your putts to the sweet spot of your putter, the more consistently energy will be transferred to your putts. Maximum energy transfer occurs when putts are impacted precisely on the putter sweet spot, and the variability in energy transfer is least sensitive when putts are struck close to the sweet spot. Drastic changes in energy transfer occur when putts are impacted far away from the putter's sweet spot.

Description

Putting results are so strongly influenced by the repeatability (or lack thereof) of impact position, that the size of a golfer's impact pattern overshadows many other individual strengths and weaknesses in putting stroke mechanics. This dependency is clearly illustrated by the correlation of the handicap vs. impact pattern size of forty-eight golfers chosen randomly from our schools (based on handicap) in Figure 3.4-2 (lower handicaps toward upper left, high handicaps toward lower right).

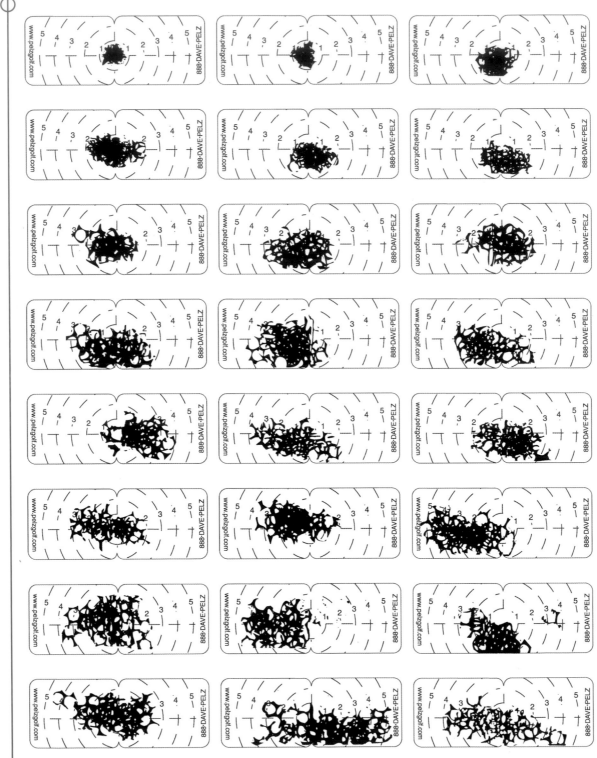

Figure 3.4-2

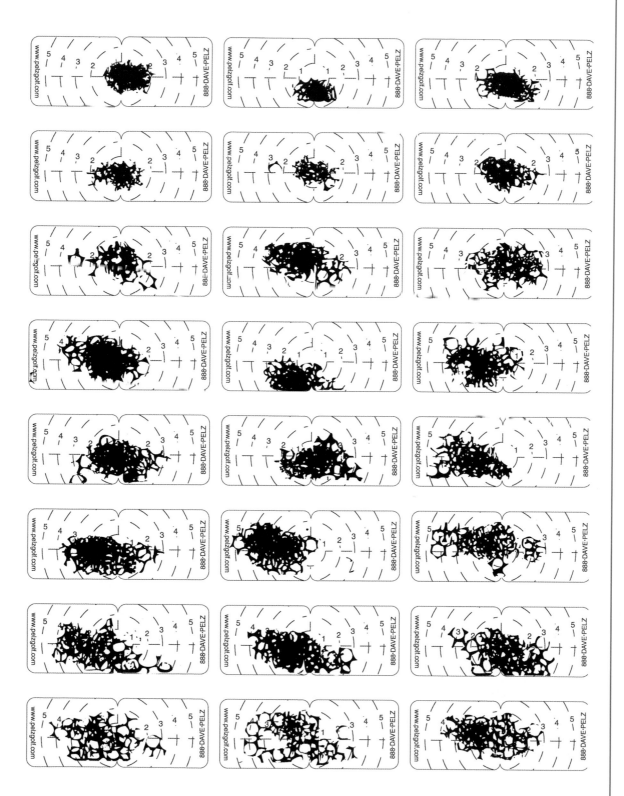

The Impact Game measures and scores your ability to strike putts on or near your putter's sweet spot, using a series of twelve putting strokes.

Alternate (in sets of two) between longer strokes (to simulate first putts on a green) and shorter strokes (similar to those you use to convert two-putts). Your six long strokes attempt to produce putts that roll approximately 25, 50, and 15 feet, each followed by second strokes meant to roll putts 6, 10, and 3 feet, respectively.

Figure 3.4-3

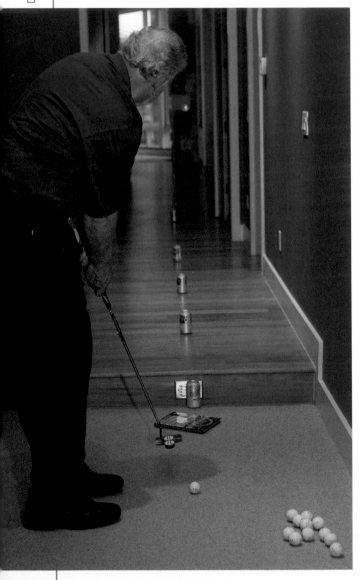

Set out target objects (Figure 3.4-3) placed at the appropriate distance from your ball as you make preview strokes, to help you make appropriate-length practice strokes.

This simulates looking at the hole during your practice strokes on the golf course.

If you use a Teacher Putter Clip (Figure 3.4-4), make sure that you've selected the appropriate tolerance for your stroke skill level (details in sidebar on the next page), and that it is centered precisely on the sweet spot of your putter.

This game rewards you (and thus trains your subconscious stroke) for impacting putts between the clip prongs.

Every time your stroke impacts a ball with a prong on your Teacher Putter Clip, you are assessed a poor-stroke penalty. The severity of the tolerance for this penalty changes with the miss/hit tolerance of the clip. The Standard clip allows the greatest miss/hit

Figure 3.4-4

margin, followed by the Pro clip, and finally the Super-Pro clip, which offers the smallest miss/hit margin.

Start each game with twelve golf balls, and putt two balls to each of six target distances (25 feet, 6 feet, 50 feet, 10 feet, 15 feet, and 3 feet).

Alternate putting between long and short putts, as mentioned earlier.

Count how many times you "prong" a putt, out of the total of twelve strokes, for your score.

How to select the proper Teacher Clip tolerance: Play your first three Impact Games with the Pro tolerance clip. If you consistently prong three or fewer of your twelve putts, you're ready to play future games with the Super-Pro clip. If you have nine or more poor putts, then go to the greater tolerance of the Standard clip. When you can consistently prong fewer than three out of twelve using a Super-Pro clip, you've achieved a PGA Tour—quality putting performance.

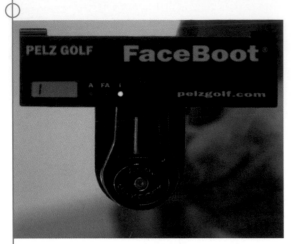

Figure 3.4-5

If you use the Face Boot-I (Figure 3.4-5) in the same game, it measures how far from the putter sweet spot (in inches) you've struck each putt.

After each putt, the device reports the miss/hit score on its bottom LCD panel. Positive scores indicate misses/hits toward the toe of the putter, while negative scores denote heel-side impacts.

The Face Boot-I steps through the same distance sequence to test your stroke on twelve putts to six distances. After the twelfth stroke it will report (by blinking) your game score, which is the average score (based on absolute values of miss/hit errors) of all twelve strokes.

How to Compete

Each player needs their own clip mounted on their putter (different clip tolerances can be used as handicaps for different skill levels).

Players alternate hitting putts (two each) to each of the distances in sequence (25 feet, 6 feet, 50 feet, 10 feet, 15 feet, 3 feet) for twelve putts total. Balls should be rolled into pillows.

Scoring is at match play, based on whether each player hits a putt solidly or "prongs" it. Ties may be carried over or not, to be mutually agreed on by the players. A game competition is for twelve holes (ties are played off in sudden death).

To play competitively with a Face Boot-I, each player must have a Face Boot mounted on his or her own putter. Both players alternate putting to each of the six Impact Game distances as above, as directed by the Face Boot-I. Putts should be rolled into pillows. Scoring is at match play, based on the impact error score of each putt. Ties may be carried over or not, to be mutually agreed on by the players (ties are played off in sudden death).

THESE GAMES ARE DIFFERENT FROM THOSE PRESENTED IN chapter 3, which involved the mechanics of your putting stroke. The games in Chapter 4 focus on what goes on in your head as you prepare for and stroke putts. In other words, they deal with your feel and touch skills.

You may have heard that putting is all mental, or that at least 99 percent of putting is mental. Of course, this is not true for all golfers, but it may in fact be accurate for a few. If you know how to read greens and have grooved a great putting stroke, but your mind won't let you pull your putter away and make that stroke, then putting is essentially all mental for you.

On the other hand, you can have the best mental approach to putting on this planet, but if your putting stroke mechanics are terrible, you probably won't be a very good putter. In this case, the mental side of your putting is not so important. Regardless of where your mental prowess rates in this overall spectrum, however, the truth is, most golfers can improve both their feel and touch. And when they do, they usually see improvement in their putting.

If you can improve your ability to (1) imagine the speed at which you want to roll 6- to 10-foot breaking putts before you stroke them (*Short-Touch Game*); (2) control touch and distance on putts between 10 and 30 feet (*Makeable-Touch and Intermediate-Touch Games*); (3) develop your lag-putting touch to minimize second-putt remainders (*Lag-Touch Game*); (4) learn to use a preview stroke to optimize your putting rhythm (*Rhythm and Preview Games*); and (5) play the games of the World Putting Championship, you will have gone a long way toward improving the entire mental side of your putting skills.

Each game provides feedback as to how well or poorly you're performing mentally at the skill in question. Remember: Your mind controls your body, your body controls your putter, and your putter controls your putting. These games will activate your mind, exercise your feel and touch for putt speed and distance, and improve your ability to coordinate what your body does relative to what your mind expects and tells it to do.

4.1
Short-Touch Game

Overview

The *Short-Touch Game* will develop your ability to match the speed of your putts to the line you've chosen. It is to be played for putts in the 6- to 10-foot range that you must start on a line aimed well above (outside of) the top edge of the hole, but that you still have a reasonable expectation to make (Figure 4.1-1).

Every golfer faces several 6- to 10-footers in every round for which they play somewhere between 6 and 10 inches of break. For these putts it's not enough to just start them on-line. To make them, you must also roll them at a speed that allows them to break the correct amount to hit the hole.

Figure 4.1-1

Description

This game consists of twelve putts breaking between 6 and 10 inches, two each from three distances in each of two different directions. Begin setup by finding a hole on a gentle slope where putts break about this amount from 8 feet.

After choosing a hole, mark three spots (with sticker-dots or tees) at 6, 8, and 10 feet, such that all three putts will break from right to left as they roll to it. Next walk to the other side of the hole and mark three more spots at the same distances for left-to-right breaking putts. Be careful to stagger the positions of the marks (as shown in Figure 4.1-2) so that no putted balls will have to roll over the footprints you make when you're hitting shorter putts.

Figure 4.1-2

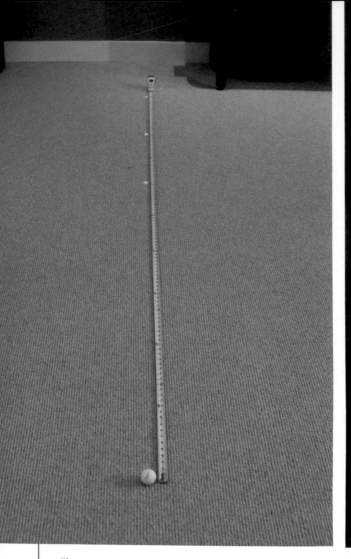

Figure 4.1-3

Figure 4.1-4

To play, you'll putt two balls from each of these six positions.

To set up this game at home, first choose a spot to putt from. Then establish the line you're going to start your putts along and place three small marks at 6 feet, 8 feet, and 10 feet on that line (sticker-dots or small pieces of tape work well, Figure 4.1-3).

Next set out three targets about six inches left and right of those marks, on both sides of your putt starting line (six targets total). These targets simulate both right-to-left and left-to-right breaking putts. And finally place a book no more than three feet in front of your putting spot (Figure 4.1-4).

Rules and Scoring

Start the Short-Touch Game by looking at the right-to-left breaking putt to the 8-foot target left of your aim line. As you make your preview stroke, imagine your putt starting on the aim line and then breaking down at perfect speed into the center of the cup. If your mind's eye is comfortable matching the stroke you just made with the vision of the roll you just imagined, you're ready to putt.

Remember, when playing games at home, duplicate what you plan to do on the golf course. By starting your putts rolling straight along your aim line, and then imagining them breaking down to the target hole or bottle, it will help transfer your practice improvements onto the course. Because even on the course, all good putting strokes start putts as though they're straight putts—they start on a straight line aimed above the hole. Putted balls then break down toward the hole from that line.

Step in, address the putt, take one last look along your line, and roll your ball by executing the exact same stroke as your preview stroke.

This is the perfect Short-Touch Game scenario: Match the feel of your practice stroke to the image of your putt starting on-line and breaking down at perfect speed into the hole. Repeat it until you get it. Make practice strokes (if you're paying attention, it shouldn't take more than three or four) until you feel the preview stroke that will hole your putt at perfect speed. Then step in and use it.

After two 8-foot putts, proceed by rolling two right-to-left breaking putts to each of the 10-foot and 6-foot targets, and six more left-to-right putts (two each) to the 8-foot, 10-foot, and 6-foot targets.

Scoring for the Short-Touch Game when it's played on a green is based on where your putts stop relative to the incoming putt line and the Optimum Putted Ball Speed Scoring Map seen in Figure 4.1-5.

OPTIMUM PUTTED BALL SPEED SCORING MAP

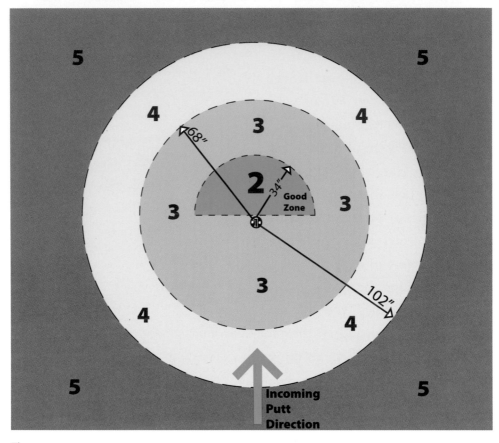

Figure 4.1-5

- Holed putts count as one stroke (1 under par)
- Good putts that roll to a stop in the "good" zone are given a par of 2 (all second putts are given)
- Poor putts that stop outside the good zone count for 3, 4, or 5, as detailed in Figure 4.1-5 above
- Minimum possible score = 12; Par score = 24; Maximum possible score = 60

The "good" zone is a semicircle with a 34-inch radius behind the back edge of the hole. Putts that stop in (or touch) the good zone have been rolled at a speed that gives them the best chance to find the hole. Your score for the game is the total of your twelve putt scores (easily remembered by keeping track of how you stand relative to par). As you can see, the lower your score for twelve putts, the better your performance.

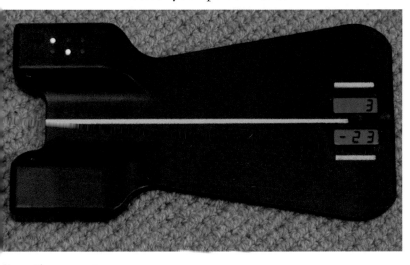

Figure 4.1-6

When the AimLine Tutor (Figure 4.1-6) is in its Short Putt (SP) game mode, it measures the initial speed and line that your putts start on, then calculates the direction and distance they would roll assuming a putt break of 8 inches on a 10-foot green-speed, perfectly smooth and sloped putting surface. It scores each putt (top LCD panel) the same as detailed earlier for playing on a practice green (Figure 4.1-6): on the basis of where it would have come to rest. It also reports how far past or short of the perfect speed (the speed that gets the ball 17 inches past the hole if the putt isn't holed) that the putt rolled (bottom LCD panel). And just as on the putting green, the minimum possible score for a 12-putt game = 12; Par score = 24; Maximum possible score = 60.

Behind every hole is a semicircular-shaped "good" zone, 34 inches in radius, that is square to the track of incoming putts and

A perfectly rolled putt is defined as a putt that rolls on-line into the center of the cup at the optimum putt speed (the speed fast enough to help a putt stay on-line and hit the hole, but not so fast as to cause too many lip-outs or to leave an excessively long second putt if it's missed).

easily measured at the end of a 35-inch putter that has its head placed down in the hole (Figure 4.1-7).

Figure 4.1-7

A putt successfully rolled at or near optimum speed will stop in the good zone behind the hole (if it doesn't go in). Putts with almost-perfect speed will stop near the center of the good zone, at a point 17 inches past the hole.

How to Compete

On a putting green: Both players alternately putt twice to the same hole from each of the three distances in each direction.

Players win or lose holes based on their putt scores (Figure 4.1-5 on page 88. The competition is at match play over twelve holes, with the winner determined by who wins the most holes (ties are played off at sudden death).

If both players score the same for a hole, the hole is halved. Play then moves on to the next hole. On most holes a measurement is not necessary, as you can usually quickly see which scoring zone each putt stopped in. Second putts are not putted out. A Short-Touch Game of twelve holes should not take more than fifteen minutes to play.

At home on a carpet: Both players alternately putt to the hole targets at distances as directed by the AimLine Tutor-SP. With two players, it is a match play competition over six holes. Holes are won or lost based on each player's score for that putt. The game winner is the player who wins the most holes out of twelve (ties are played off at sudden death).

4.2
Makeable-Touch Game

> Putts rolling at optimum speed as they approach a hole will roll 17 inches past it, on average, if they miss the cup.

Overview

The intent of the *Makeable-Touch Game* is to improve your ability to hole putts in the very makeable 10- to 20-foot range. The game trains you to maximize your make percentage by rolling putts at the optimum speed: fast enough to stay on-line and hit the hole, but slow enough to minimize lip-outs.

Description

This game consists of two cycles of six putts (twelve total), with each cycle composed of two putts from each of three distances. You can play this game on a practice green outdoors, or indoors with a Touch Tutor learning aid. There is a semicircular-shaped "good" zone, 34 inches in radius, behind the hole (Figure 4.2-1, as measured with a 38-inch putter).

Figure 4.2-1

On a practice green: First choose a hole and mark off putts of 15, 20, and 10 feet (Figure 4.2-2).

Figure 4.2-2

Walk three large steps straight away from the hole and stick a tee in the green about 12 inches past your farthest foot (Figure 4.2-3) to mark a 10-foot distance from the cup.

Figure 4.2-3

Take two more big steps in the same direction and place a tee behind your farthest foot for the 15-foot marker, and finally walk another two steps plus one foot for a 20-foot putt to the hole.

Each time you play this game, walk in different directions from the hole you choose, so over time you'll putt uphill, downhill, and sidehill putts. To play the Makeable-Touch Game, you'll putt two balls from each of three distances (15 feet first, then 20 feet and 10 feet), as marked. Then repeat the same cycle a second time.

Scoring for the Makeable-Touch Game is shown in Figure 4.2-4.

OPTIMUM PUTTED BALL SPEED SCORING MAP

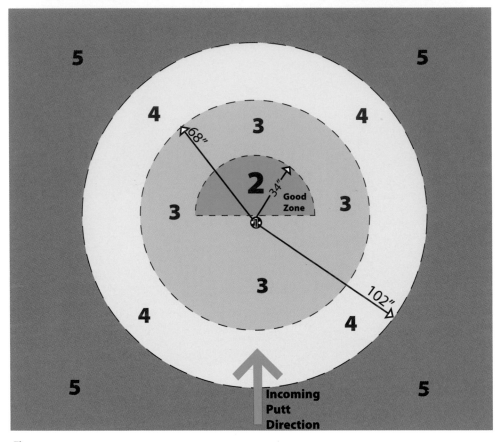

Figure 4.2-4

- Holed putts = 1
- Putts that do not go in, but stop in or touch the "good" zone = 2 (all second putts are given)
- Putts that miss the good zone but stop within 68 inches of the hole = 3
- Putts that stop between 68 and 102 inches = 4
- Putts that stop more than 102 inches from the hole = 5
- Minimum possible score for 12-putt game = 12; Par score = 24; Maximum possible score = 60

Your score for the game is the total of twelve putt scores. The lower your score, the better your performance.

At home with the Touch Tutor-A:
Select a position from which you're going to putt and place the Touch Tutor-A (Figure 4.2-5) there.

Set the Touch Tutor into its Makeable-Putt Game mode (A), and aim the white aim line in the desired putting direction. With three targets in your hands, walk

Figure 4.2-5

off the three makeable-putt distances of 10 feet, 15 feet, and 20 feet and place a target at each distance. These targets are for you to look at during your practice strokes—they will help make this game experience as realistic and meaningful as possible, so that it will transfer to your on-course putting later. Place a blocking pillow in front of your Touch Tutor-A so that putted balls don't hit the targets and move them (Figure 4.2-6).

Figure 4.2-6

At home, scoring is accomplished when the Touch Tutor-A measures the distance each putt would have rolled on a 10-foot green-speed, perfectly level putting green. Scoring is based on the same system detailed earlier (Figure 4.2-4).

The putt score appears after each putt on the top LCD panel, and a second number is also reported on the lower LCD. This is the putt miss-distance (measured in inches of roll) from the "perfect" putt speed. Positive numbers measure how far past perfect your ball

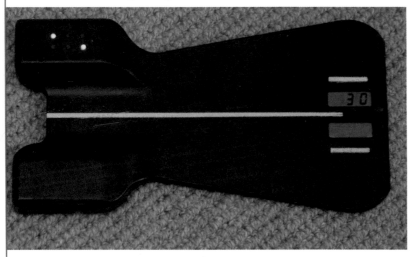

would have rolled; negative numbers mean how far short of perfect it rolled. Both the putt score and miss-distance measurements stay on the LCD readouts for approximately seven seconds (Figure 4.2-7).

After your twelfth

Figure 4.2-7

putt the Touch Tutor-A will report your twelfth putt score and miss-distance, and then automatically switch to displaying your game score in two ways:

Score #1 (top LCD—flashing) = Total Game Score (total of twelve putt scores).

Score #2 (bottom LCD—flashing) = average miss-distance for game.

How to Compete

On a putting green, both players putt alternately to the same holes from the lengths of 15 feet, 20 feet, and 10 feet. Players win or lose holes based on putt scores (detailed in Figure 4.2-4). The competition is at match play over twelve holes, with the winner determined by who wins the most holes out of twelve (ties are played off at sudden death).

On most holes a measurement is not necessary, as you can usually quickly see which score each putt deserves. Second putts are not putted out, because you're trying to emphasize your ability to hole makeable-length putts, not to work on your short-putt stroke.

To compete at home, each of two players putts one ball at each distance as the Touch Tutor-A steps through the makeable-putt distances. The match proceeds as above (as though you were playing on a putting green), with one player winning a hole if his or her putt scores better than their opponent's putt scores to the same target. When both players' putts score the same, the hole is tied.

The competition is at match play over six holes, with the winner determined by who wins the most holes out of six (ties are played off at sudden death).

Note: In a game competition using one Touch Tutor-A, the final total miss-distance after twelve putts is not used, because it measures the combined errors of both players and is meaningless in the competition.

4.3
Intermediate-Touch Game

Overview

The intent of the *Intermediate-Touch Game* is to improve your ability to hole an occasional putt in the 20- to 30-foot range, while at the same time minimizing your chances of three-putting. The game trains you to roll putts at the optimum putt speed.

Description

The Intermediate-Touch Game consists of twelve putts, to be putted in two cycles of 2/2/2 putts from each of three intermediate-length distances: 25, 30, and 20 feet (Figure 4.3-1).

Figure 4.3-1

For both ways to play this game (outdoors on a putting green, indoors with a learning aid), there is always a "good" zone behind the hole into which well-struck putts roll and stop.

On a practice green, first choose a hole to putt to and walk off seven large steps straight away from it. Place a marker (sticker-dot or tee) on the green behind your farthest foot to mark 20 feet from the hole.

Then walk another two big steps in the same direction and place a second marker behind your farthest foot (25 feet from the cup).

Finally walk another two steps and mark a spot behind your farthest foot for a 30-foot putt.

For each game you play, you'll putt two balls from each of the three distances (two from 25 feet, two from 30 feet, and two from 20 feet) to the chosen hole. Then you'll repeat the cycle.

Scoring for the Intermediate-Touch Game is determined by where the putts stop relative to the Optimum Putted Ball Speed Scoring Map, as seen in Figure 4.3-2.

OPTIMUM PUTTED BALL SPEED SCORING MAP

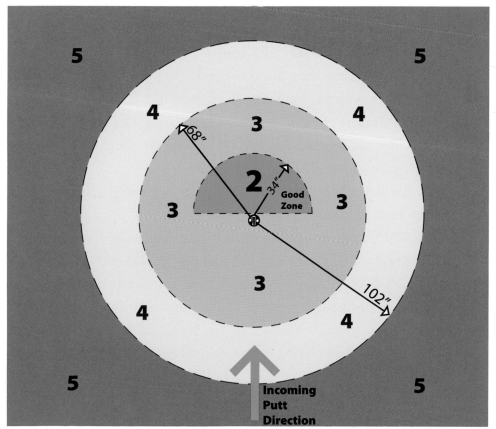

Figure
4.3-2

- Holed putts = 1
- Putts that do not go in, but stop in or touch the "good" zone = 2 (all second putts are given)
- Putts that stop outside the good zone but within 68 inches of the hole = 3
- Putts that stop between 68 and 102 inches from the hole = 4
- Putts that stop more than 102 inches from the hole = 5
- Minimum possible score for game = 12; Par score = 24; Maximum possible score = 60

Figure 4.3-3

Your score for the game is the total of your twelve putt scores.

To play indoors at home with a Touch Tutor-EE (in its Intermediate Touch Game mode = EE), select the position from which you plan to putt and place the Touch Tutor-EE (Figure 4.3-3) on that spot.

Carefully aim the white aim line in the putting direction. Walk off three intermediate-putt distances of 20 feet, 25 feet, and 30 feet, placing a target at each distance. These targets are for you to look at during your pre-putt practice stroke, to make the game experience as realistic and meaningful as possible.

Place a ball on the Touch Tutor-EE tee and prepare to make your first practice stroke.

Make a preview stroke while looking at the 25-foot target.

Then address your first ball and putt it with a 25-foot stroke. The ball does not have to roll 25 feet or any significant distance (it should be putted into a pillow directly in front of you as shown in Figure 4.3-4).

In fact, when playing this game indoors, it's better to not watch the ball roll at all.

After you putt the first ball, the Touch Tutor-EE will measure

Figure
4.3-4

the distance the ball would have rolled on a 10-foot green-speed, perfectly level putting green. This distance is compared to the "perfect" distance you were trying to roll this putt—either into the hole or at least into the good zone behind the hole. The upper LCD panel

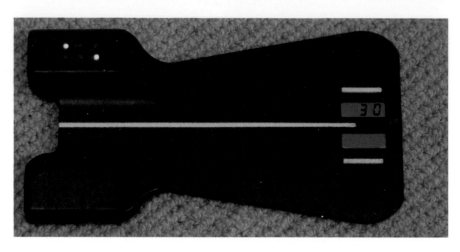

Figure 4.3-5

then reads out the putt score for that putt (Figure 4.3-5), while the lower LCD panel displays the miss-distance from the perfect putt distance.

After your twelfth putt the Touch Tutor-EE will report your twelfth putt score and miss-distance, then automatically switch to displaying your final game score in two ways:

Score #1 (top LCD) = Game score (sum of twelve putt scores)
Score #2 (bottom LCD) = Game average miss-distances (absolute values)

How to Compete

On a putting green, two players alternately putt from lengths of 25 feet, 20 feet, and 30 feet, twice from each distance, with putt scoring as detailed earlier (Figure 4.3-2), then repeat the cycle of six putts each.

Remember that the "good" zone is one putter length behind the hole (measure with a putter marked at 34 inches), oriented perpendicular to the incoming direction of the putt.

The competition is at match play based on putt scores over 12 holes, with the winner determined by who wins the most holes (ties are played off at sudden death).

To play at home using a Touch Tutor-EE, both players alternately putt twice from each of three intermediate-putt distances as the Touch Tutor-EE steps through them.

Then both repeat the cycle a second time. The match proceeds as though they were playing on a putting green, with one player winning a hole when his putt score to the same target is lower than his opponent's.

The competition is match play over six holes, the winner determined by who wins the most holes (ties are played off at sudden death). Note. The final total miss-distance after twelve putts cannot be used, as it is a measurement of the combined errors of both players and is meaningless in terms of the competition.

4.4
Lag-Touch Game

Overview

The intent of the *Lag-Touch Game* is to improve your ability to lag your long putts of 35 feet or more close to the hole. It establishes three reference lag distances of 40, 50, and 60 feet and trains you to putt them accurately. The concept is that once you develop a good touch for these reference putts, you'll also be good from slightly shorter and longer distances. This will also lead to direct improvement in avoiding the frequent three-putts that golfers experience from lag-putt distances.

Description

The Lag-Touch Game consists of twelve lag putts (two cycles of two putts from each of the three reference distances), with your score determined by how close your putts stop to the hole. Whether lag-putting outdoors on a practice green or indoors with a learning aid, the "good" zone is a circle with a 34-inch radius surrounding the hole (Figure 4.4-1).

This good zone is the target, rather than the hole or past the hole, into which all players should be trying to roll long putts. It provides the centerpiece of a metric for measuring the quality of lag-putting.

Although sometimes you'll want to lag up-, down-, or sidehill across the slope of a green, it is important to always putt from the

Figure
4.4-1

same three reference distances of 50 feet, 60 feet, and 40 feet. They are the most frequent distances that you'll face on the course, and the distances you want to "own" and adjust from for all other long putts.

To play on a practice green (Figure 4.4-2), choose a hole, walk thirteen large steps plus one foot length straight away from the hole in the direction you want to putt, and mark (with a sticker-dot or tee) a 40-foot distance from the cup.

Then move a step straight sideways and walk another three steps plus one foot in the same direction and place another marker at 50 feet. Look back and make sure you won't have to putt over your footprints from the 40-foot putts when you putt from this 50-foot mark.

Then step sideways again and walk another three steps plus one foot away from the hole, and place the third reference putt marker at 60 feet.

Figure
4.4-2

These three markers establish the reference distances for the Lag-Touch Game. For each game you'll start with a six-putt cycle, two from each of the three reference markers to the chosen hole.

Then repeat the cycle one more time, putting twelve balls for a complete game.

Figure 4.4-3

To play at home on a carpet with the Touch Tutor-LAG in its Lag-Putt Game mode (LAG) (Figure 4.4-3), select the position from which you are going to putt, set the Touch Tutor into its "LAG" mode, and aim its aim line along the intended putting direction line. Place a Phony Hole (or can or bottle) at each of the three reference distances of 40 feet, 50 feet, and 60 feet down a hallway as markers (Figure 4.4-4).

Figure 4.4-4

Place a ball on the Touch Tutor and after a good preview stroke, putt it to the 50-foot target. The ball should roll into a pillow directly in front of you as shown in Figure 4.4-5.

It's better not to watch the ball's unrealistic roll indoors.

After two putts to each of the three reference distances, repeat all six putts in the same order a second time for a full twelve-putt game.

Figure 4.4-5

Figure 4.4-6

The Touch Tutor will measure the distance your ball would have rolled on a perfectly level putting green of 10-foot green-speed, and report the score of your stroke relative to your target distance of 50 feet on its top LCD (for a scoring map, see Figure 4.4-7 below). It will also report the miss-distance of your putt relative to your 50-foot target on the bottom LCD (Figure 4.4-6).

Scoring is different from the Makeable (A)- and Intermediate (EE)-Touch Games, because the "good" putt zone fully surrounds the hole for the lag (LAG) putting game as shown in Figure 4.4-7.

LAG PUTTING SCORING MAP

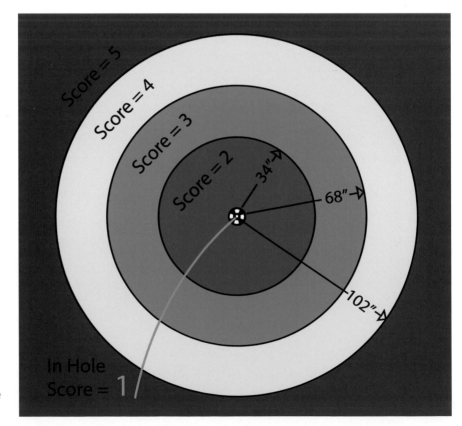

Figure 4.4-7

The difference is that putts left short of, but close to, the hole are "good" in lag-putting (the main point being to NOT three-putt). Lag-Touch Game scoring is the same for indoor vs. outdoor play as follows:

- Holed putts = 1
- Putts that stop in or touch the "good" zone 34 inches around the hole = 2 (all second putts are given)
- Putts that miss the good zone but stop within 68 inches of the hole = 3
- Putts that stop between 68 and 102 inches from the hole = 4
- Putts that stop more than 102 inches from the hole = 5
- Minimum possible score = 12; Par score = 24; Maximum possible score = 60

How to Compete

To compete on a putting green, players alternately putt twice from each of the three reference distances (50 feet, 60 feet, and 40 feet), then repeat the cycle for a twelve-hole game. And remember: On long, lag putts of over 35 feet in length, the "good" putt-zone circle of one putter length radius (34 inches) completely surrounds all the way around the hole (is not just behind the hole as in the Makeable- and Intermediate-Touch Games), as shown using one player's 35-inch putter in Figure 4.4-8.

Figure 4.4-8

The competition scoring is based on each player's putt scores. The game winner is determined by who wins the most holes out of twelve (ties after twelve holes are played off at sudden death).

If both players score the same, the hole is halved. On most holes a measurement is not necessary, because you can usually quickly see which scoring zone each putt has come to rest in. Second putts are not putted out, because you're trying to emphasize your ability to lag putts close to the hole, not to work on your short putts.

To compete at home, both players putt one ball at each distance as the Touch Tutor-LAG steps through the lag-putt distances. The match proceeds as above (as though they were playing on a putting green), with one player winning a hole if his putt score is lower. When both players' putt scores are the same, the hole is tied.

The competition is at match play over six holes, with the winner determined by winning the most holes out of six (ties are played off at sudden death). The final average miss-distance is not used, as it combines errors of both players and is meaningless in terms of the competition.

4.5
Feel-for-Speed Game

Overview

The intent of the *Feel-for-Speed Game* is to enhance your ability to "feel" small differences in speed that your strokes impart to putts. This is accomplished by engaging you in many repetitions of a single "speed-critical" putt, while simultaneously providing you with feedback to fine-tune your mind and body's speed-control muscles.

The ultimate goal remains to improve your ability to hole more putts on the golf course. But this game specifically targets your feel for speed, as distinct from other games that develop your stroke mechanics or ability to aim. The Feel-for-Speed Game gets you dialed-in and totally focused on feeling the precision speed control required to maximize your ability to hole putts.

Description

Each game consists of twelve identical putts from 15 feet, 20 feet, or 10 feet. You select which distance to putt to each time you play a game. For either of the two ways you can play this game—on a practice putting green with a Phony Hole, or indoors with an Aim-Line Tutor-FFS (in its FFS or Feel-for-Speed mode) learning aid—there will be a putt score for every putt rolled.

To play outdoors on a practice green, you need to find seriously breaking putts. The more a putt breaks on its way to the hole, the more its line depends on the speed at which it rolls. Therefore, to play the Feel-for-Speed Game you must find a putt of 10 feet, 15 feet, or 20 feet that breaks at least 12 inches but not more than 36 inches.

Walk around the putting green and find an area of smooth but signifi-cantly sloped green surface (not a se-vere tier between two green levels). You need a Phony Hole (Figure 4.5-1) that your ball can roll right over, in-stead of a real hole.

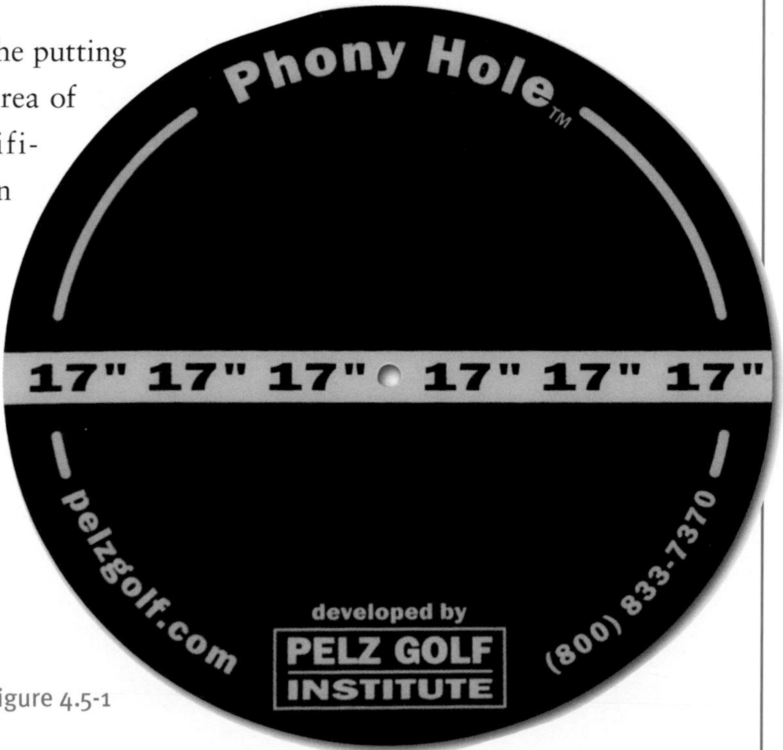

Figure 4.5-1

Assuming you've chosen to practice from 15 feet, lay the Phony Hole on the green and casually roll several 15-foot putts at it from different directions. When you find a putt that breaks at least 12 inches on what you consider to be a green-slope area that's acceptable as a location for a hole (Figure 4.5-2), you've found the putt you can use to play the Feel-for-Speed Game.

After you choose the putt direction and Phony Hole location, place one sticker-dot marker at the 15-foot distance you want to putt from and another precisely at the end of the extended putt line 17 inches past the Phony Hole, which is where you expect

Figure 4.5-2

the perfect optimum-speed putt to come to rest (Figure 4.5-3).

To play a Feel-for-Speed Game, you're going to putt twelve times from the exact same spot on the green. Your perfect putt will roll over the center of the Phony Hole and stop on the sticker-dot 17 inches behind the hole's back edge.

The Phony Hole is required for this game so you can see how far putts that would normally be made would roll past the hole before stopping. A real hole can't be used because it stops the ball and eliminates the feedback needed to judge how near to optimum speed the ball was rolling as it approached the hole.

Figure 4.5-3

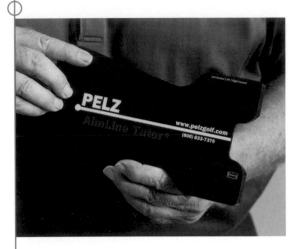

Figure 4.5-4

Figure 4.5-5

To play indoors with the AimLine Tutor-FFS (Figure 4.5-4), place the AimLine Tutor-FFS on the spot you want to putt from and carefully aim the white aim line at a starting-line target at the distance you've selected for your breaking putts. Now place a hole target (Phony Hole, bottle, or can) at least 12 inches off to the left or right of the aim line out at your desired putt length (Figure 4.5-5), to simulate the hole your putts will break to. Also place a pillow 2 feet along your aim line to stop your putted balls.

Place a ball on the AimLine Tutor-FFS and prepare to make your first practice stroke (having eleven more balls close by will be convenient).

Make a preview practice stroke while looking out along your aim line and imagining your putt curving over to your target. Then address the ball and putt it. The ball does not have to roll any significant distance—it should stop in the pillow directly in front of you (it's best not to watch the ball roll, since it's not really going to break on the indoor surface anyway).

To score on a putting green, each putt is scored according to the Optimum Putted Ball Speed Scoring Map, as detailed in Figure 4.5-6.

OPTIMUM PUTTED BALL SPEED SCORING MAP

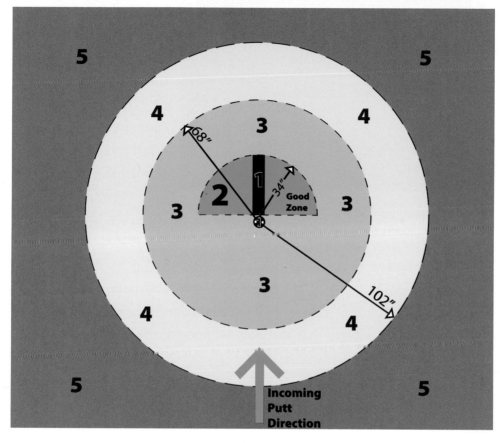

Figure
4.5-6

"Made" putts (score = 1) are those that roll at least one-half of the ball over the Phony Hole and stop in the good zone (34-inch-deep semicircle) behind it. A score of 2 is given to putts that miss the Phony Hole but stop in the goodspeed zone. Putts that stop outside of (not touching) the good zone but within 68 inches of, between 68 and 102 inches from, or more than 102 inches from the Phony Hole receive scores of 3, 4, and 5, respectively.

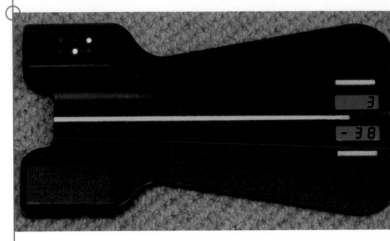

Figure 4.5-7

To score with an Aim-Line Tutor-FFS: The Aim-Line Tutor-FFS measures how close to the perfect line and speed each ball rolled, then reports its score based on that roll relative to Figure 4.5-6 (assuming a 10-foot green-speed and a 12-inch break). This score is shown in the LCD panel above the ball (Figure 4.5-7).

Shown in the LCD panel below the ball is each putt's miss-distance short or long of the perfect distance, 17 inches past the hole. Positive numbers indicate that the putt rolled too far, while negative numbers indicate that the putt stopped short of the perfect roll distance.

After your twelfth putt score and distance error are reported, your game scores are then reported in two ways:

> **Score #1** (top LCD) will flash your Total Game Score (the total of your twelve putt scores).
> **Score #2** (bottom LCD) will show (by blinking) your game miss-distance (the average of absolute values).

How to Compete

On a green, the Feel-for-Speed Game competition is match play over twelve consecutive putts by each player (players putt alternately) to the same hole (Figure 4.5-8).

The winner of each hole is the player whose putt rolls over the Phony Hole and stops closest to the perfect (17 inches past) "sticker-dot." The winner is the player who wins the most holes out of twelve (ties after twelve holes are played off at sudden death).

Figure 4.5-8

To compete at home using an AimLine Tutor-FFS, players putt alternately down the same aim line to the target distance selected on the Tutor. Both players putt at the same right-to-left or left-to-right target, with the lower putt score winning.

The competition is at match play over six holes, and the game winner is the player who wins the most holes (the final average miss-distance reported after twelve putts is not used, as it measures the combined errors of both players and is meaningless for competition purposes).

4.6
Rhythm Game

Overview

The intent of the *Rhythm Game* is to enhance your ability to consistently make smooth, rhythmic, and accelerating putting strokes. The smoother and more rhythmic your natural putting stroke becomes, the easier it is to repeat its motion. And an accelerating putter is far more stable through the impact zone of a putting stroke than a decelerating putter.

A fundamental of the Rhythm Game is to learn the feel of rhythmically and repeatedly accelerating through the impact zone of your putting stroke.

Description

If a golfer uses the same stroke motion to putt a ball as he does in his perfect practice stroke, the ball impact disrupts the smooth acceleration in the forward-stroke motion. At the point of this interruption, an accelerating putter always produces more consistent and superior putting results than it would if it had been decelerating into impact.

In a perfect practice stroke, a putter should smoothly speed up and then slow to a stop in the backswing. During the forward swing, the putter should again smoothly accelerate until it is past the expected impact with the ball, then smoothly slow to a stop again. In the forward motion of a perfect practice stroke, the stroke length after ball impact should be slightly greater than the stroke length prior to impact (Figure 4.6-1).

←backswing→ | ← follow through →

Center
of stroke motion

Figure 4.6-1

The Rhythm Game consists of trying to make twelve perfect practice strokes (each of which follows the same theoretically perfect stroke-acceleration profile) to three different putt lengths. The game is played indoors on a carpet (or a synthetic putting surface), and players putt toward targets set out at the proper distances with a Stroke Boot-R (set into its Rhythm Game mode = R) learning aid attached to your putter (Figure 4.6-2).

Figure 4.6-2

The benefits of having a rhythmic and stable (accelerating) stroke through impact are evident in the roll consistency of your putts for all putt lengths. Initially, however, the most improvement in putting results can be achieved by playing rhythm games in the short and makeable (6- to 20-foot) putt ranges.

To set up for a Rhythm Game, mark off the three putt lengths (6 feet, 12 feet, and 20 feet) and place a target Phony Hole (bottle or can) to simulate a hole at each distance. Then attach the Stroke Boot to your putter and set it to the Rhythm (R) game mode. Set up to the twelve-foot putt (Figure 4.6-3) as though you're going to make

Figure 4.6-3

a practice stroke before you putt it. You're now ready to start the Rhythm Game by trying to make "perfect-rhythm" practice strokes.

Each practice stroke will be measured and scored while you simply focus on your stroke rhythm. The Stroke Boot-R learning aid constantly monitors whether your putter is increasing or decreasing its speed throughout your stroke. After four practice strokes to the 12-foot target, look to the 20-foot target and make four practice strokes to it. This is followed by four strokes to the 6-foot target, for a Rhythm Game of twelve strokes.

Rules and Scoring

A Rhythm Game consists of twelve individual practice strokes (without any real strokes that putt the ball), four each at three different length putts. As you make strokes, the Stroke Boot-R will measure and audibly identify ("beep") when your putterhead reaches maximum velocity (speed) and starts to slow down in your stroke's forward motion. If this beep occurs before the impact position in your stroke, your putter has decelerated into its impact position, and the Tutor would rate that effort as "poor." If the beep occurs after your putter passes the ball (impact position), however, then you've accelerated through the impact zone and your stroke is considered "good."

Figure 4.6-4

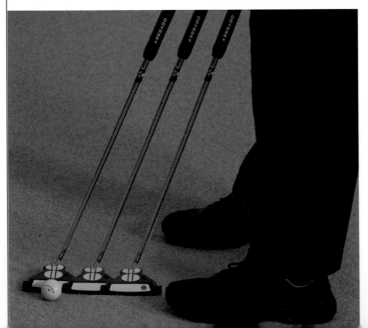

To play, you must notify the Stroke Boot-R that you are ready to start making real practice strokes. This is done by moving the putterhead from its position just behind the ball straight back toward your feet and then straight back out toward the ball, as shown in Figure 4.6-4.

Now the Stroke Boot-R is ready to measure your stroke motion as you make practice strokes to your target. You're never actually going to step in and putt the ball. Simply take four practice strokes while aiming at the twelve-foot target. Then turn your attention to the 20-foot target and make four more practice strokes. Then make four practice strokes to your 6-foot target. The purpose of the Rhythm Game is to focus on smoothness, rhythm, and the timing of your stroke's maximum velocity beep during each of these twelve practice strokes.

After each stroke the Stroke Boot-R reads out a score based on the timing difference between its rhythm and a theoretically perfect stroke. A score of zero means perfect rhythm and timing in your stroke. A positive score means that max velocity came too late in your stroke, while a negative score indicates that you reached max velocity too early relative to perfect timing. (Note: LCD panel readings are visible from a floor mirror provided with the Stroke Boot.)

To play the Rhythm Game: The Stroke Boot-R's (Figure 4.6-5) primary feedback is the real-time audible "beep" at the time of maximum putterhead speed in each stroke.

Its secondary feedback is the timing (plus or minus, Figure 4.6-6) of the beep relative to the "perfect" timing of the max-velocity beep in a theoretically perfect putting stroke motion. Again, positive numbers mean that your max stroke speed is coming too late in your stroke—you're accelerating for too long after impact and you should try to smooth out your stroke (in other words, be less aggressive) in future strokes.

Figure 4.6-5

If your stroke scores are negative, it means that your putter is reaching top speed too early in your forward stroke—your backswing

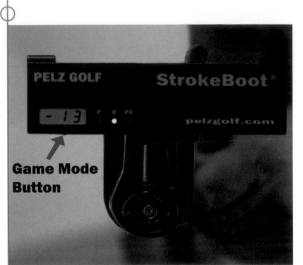

Game Mode Button

Figure 4.6-6

may be too long—and your putter is decelerating when it arrives at impact. To correct this, you need to be more aggressive, take a shorter backswing, and make a longer follow-through.

The Stroke Boot also provides a flashing display of your game score after your twelfth practice stroke. The game score is your average max-velocity timing error for twelve strokes, which relates to your stroke consistency.

As you develop your stroke rhythm, please understand that perfect-rhythm strokes don't make all putts. Holing putts also depends on your green-reading abilities, stroke mechanics, and touch and feel for proper putt speed. However, you can rest assured: The better you develop your stroke rhythm, the more putts you'll make over the long haul.

How to Compete

Both players must have Stroke Boots attached to their putters.

Each player should have their own three targets set out and make practice strokes alternately while looking at the same target distances. After each stroke, the player who achieves the better stroke score is the winner. The winner of the game is the player who wins the most holes (practice strokes) out of twelve. The winner of a tie game after twelve strokes is determined by the player with the lowest (smallest) average timing error in their maximum putterhead speed.

4.7
Preview-Stroke Game

Overview

The purpose of the *Preview-Stroke Game* is to help you develop the skill of using the exact same stroke to putt your ball that you've just seen and felt in your final practice (preview) stroke. The preview stroke is the stroke that your mind's eye judged to be perfect for the putt you're facing. If you develop the focus and discipline to create a great preview stroke, and can use it immediately thereafter as your real putting stroke, you can be a great putter!

Description

It is one thing to have the ability to "feel" the stroke you want to make before putting. It is quite another to have the mental focus to be able to use that exact same feel and stroke to actually roll your putt under pressure. It is this second skill—the ability to repeat your preview stroke when you actually roll your putts—that playing the Preview-Stroke Game will develop.

The intent of the game is simple. Learn to repeat your preview stroke, with the exact same feel and rhythm, when you make your real putting stroke. You'll be amazed at how much easier this makes putting under pressure, and how much your putting will improve once you develop this skill.

The Preview-Stroke Game is played indoors on a carpet (or a synthetic putting surface), with a Stroke Boot learning aid, set in the Preview (PV) mode, attached to your putter (Figure 4.7-1).

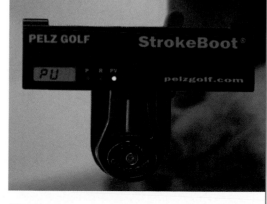

Figure 4.7-1

The Preview-Stroke Game requires that you make four pairs of strokes (one preview followed by one real stroke makes a pair) at three different putt lengths: four each at 12 feet, four more at 20 feet, and four stroke pairs at 6 feet. For every stroke pair that you make, the Stroke Boot-PV will measure and store the rhythm profile of each preview stroke and then compare it to the profile of your real stroke.

First, select a spot to putt from and set targets out along your aim line at three distances (6 feet, 12 feet, and 20 feet). Place a pillow three feet in front of your ball (so you won't see unrealistic rolls) if you are putting on a bumpy, uneven, or sloped surface. As seen in Figure 4.7-2, I'm ready to address my ball in a practice stroke position, perhaps 3 or 4 inches farther away from the ball than I would be in my normal putting position, on a perfect rolling SYNLawn putting carpet.

Figure 4.7-2

Make as many practice strokes as you like as you dial-in your feel for the stroke you want to make. When your mind's eye sees and feels that you've made the stroke you want, you're ready to start the game.

You must first alert the Stroke Boot-PV with a trigger by pulling the putter straight away from the ball toward your toe line (as shown in Figure 4.7-3). This motion tells the device that you're about to make your preview stroke.

Figure 4.7-3

The Stroke Boot-PV looks for a putterhead motion perpendicular to your putting stroke path as its trigger to start measuring velocity profiles. Don't move your putter this way unless you're ready to make a good preview stroke followed immediately by a real stroke.

The Preview-Stroke Game sequence for one pair of strokes is as follows:

ONE PAIR OF STROKES IN PREVIEW GAME

1. As many practice strokes as you want until you're ready to make your preview stroke.
2. Pull the trigger by moving your putter toward your toes then back toward the ball.
3. Make your final practice stroke your preview stroke.
4. Move in, address the ball, and execute your real putting stroke.

The Stroke Boot-PV will measure the difference in rhythm between your last practice preview stroke and your real stroke and report your "preview-repeatability" score on its LCD panel. To complete the game you must complete four pairs of preview/real strokes to each of three distances: 12 feet, 20 feet, and 6 feet.

Rules and Scoring

In the Preview (PV) mode, the Stroke Boot steps through three different putt distances. You'll quickly learn at which putt length your stroke is most repeatable. Your preview-repeatability score will always range between 0 (zero error for a perfectly repeated preview stroke) and 999 (the worst possible repetition score = completely non-repeatable).

Your flashing Preview-Stroke Game score, displayed after your twelfth stroke-pair score, will be the average of your twelve previous scores. Don't ever be discouraged by this score. This is a new concept in putting improvement that most golfers have never thought of before, or ever practiced. By simply concentrating on making the same real putting stroke as you have felt in your preview stroke, your stroke rhythm repeatability scores will improve with practice (as will your putting on the course). I promise.

How to Compete

Both players must have a Stroke Boot-PV attached to their putter. The game is at match play and both players must alternately address their practice stroke positions for each of their twelve stroke pairs.

Both players must putt alternately to the same target distance as directed by their Stroke Boots.

After each competitor makes a practice/real stroke pair, the player who achieves the lowest (best) repeatability score is the winner of that hole (stroke pair). If both players receive the same rating, the hole is halved. The winner of a tie game is determined by the player with the lowest average repeatability score.

4.8
Games of the World
Putting Championship®

The World Putting Championship® (WPC®) is an annual competition designed to identify and crown the world's best putter. I have personally designed and run this competition twice, and hope to continue it in the future.

The games of the WPC are designed to test how well golfers putt over the full distribution of putt lengths normally encountered when playing a large number of 18-hole rounds. The putt lengths duplicate these same putt lengths and measure not only each player's ability to hole putts and avoid three-putting, but also their ability to roll putts at or near optimum speeds when their ball fails to find the hole.

All putting and putters in WPC games must conform to the USGA rules of golf, with special competition exceptions to help determine the best putter. There are four different games that make up the competition. The first game is medal play (your score is the number of strokes you take), with players putting as they do in most tournaments you see on television or at your home course.

The other three games are scientifically designed to test specific aspects of putting. Drawback, Safety Drawback, and Double Safety Drawback test players' abilities over differing lengths of putts. While Drawback emphasizes a player's ability to lag or "die" long putts near the hole, it also tests the player's ability to hole drawn-back putts in the 6- to 12-foot range. Safety Drawback is designed to measure a player's ability to hole putts in makeable- and intermediate-putt lengths from 10 feet to 30 feet, as well as their ability to follow up and hole the drawn-back putts in the 4- to 8-foot range. Double Safety Drawback measures the speed control and touch of a player in the makeable-putt length range between 10 feet and 20 feet, as well as putts in the 9- to 15-foot range.

The rules detailed in Figures 4.8-1, -2, and -3 below, have a common theme. The golfer is rewarded or penalized on the length of his second putt, based on the quality of where the first putt stops if it doesn't go into the hole.

Rules for Drawback (Figure 4.8-1)

For example, in good putting, long lag putts should stop hole-high and as close to the hole as possible. Short but close is good in lag putting, because the primary goal of a good lag putt is to *not* three-putt. If the putt has a chance to luck in, that's fine—but don't three-putt. In playing Drawback for putts longer than 30 feet, the closer to the hole the first putt stops, the better. When a first putt stops in or touching the "safe" zone (within a radius of 34 inches surrounding the hole), it is exempt from drawback and is to be putted out from where it stopped. If it stops outside the "safe" zone, it must be drawn back (have 34 inches added to it) before it is putted again. All missed second or later putts are drawn back 34 inches from the hole before being putted again. This way, Drawback also tests your ability to both hole 4- to 12-foot putts and lag your long ones close.

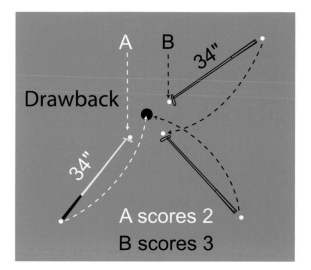

Figure 4.8-1

Rules for Safety Drawback (Figure 4.8-2)

In Safety Drawback, which is played for putts from 10 feet to 30 feet, all second (and subsequent) putts are drawn back radially away from the hole by 34 inches before they are putted, except for first putts that go into the hole or stop in the safe zone. The golfer is thus rewarded not only for holing first putts, but also for rolling putts at or near the optimum speed. His or her ability to hole 2- to 7-footers is also tested.

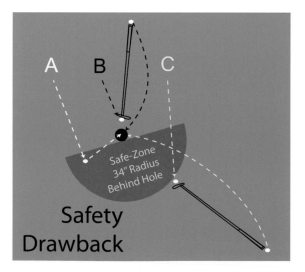

Figure 4.8-2

Rules for Double Safety Drawback (Figure 4.8-3)

And finally, Double Safety Drawback is similar to Safety Drawback, except that it is played for initial putts between 7 and 15 feet, and it's twice as penal (drawback distance is two putter lengths, or 68 inches instead of 34 inches). This puts extreme pressure on the golfer to roll his/her first putt at or near optimum speed, and tests them on 9- to 15-foot next putts when they don't.

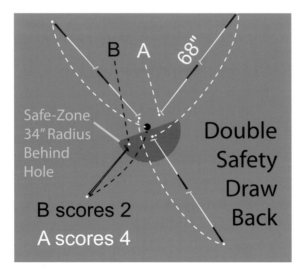

Figure 4.8-3

AT THIS POINT YOU KNOW ABOUT OUR GAMES TO EVALUATE your putting skills, games to improve your stroke mechanics, and games to develop your feel and touch for speed and distance. You also know about the new learning aids that will help you improve in the convenience of your own home. In fact, you're ready to start playing the games that will get you on your way to improving your putting skills. But first I'd like to make three quick points that don't seem to fit anywhere else in your improvement program.

First, not all putting games will improve your putting; there are some you shouldn't play. Second, I want to discuss the vehement dislike that some golfers have for learning aids. And third, I want to bring you up-to-date on my research on green-reading.

5.1
Two Games You Shouldn't Play

As detailed in Chapter 1.3, playing games with good feedback on your results is crucial to improving your putting. But there are a few putting games that give you bad feedback and end up hurting your putting. It may sound like an old cliché, but it's true: Bad feedback is worse than no feedback.

The two games I recommend that you don't play are "Aces" and "Putting to the Small Hole." I'll talk about Aces first.

The Game of Aces

In a game of Aces, each competitor putts to the chosen hole in a match play format. If both players make or miss the first putt, the hole is tied and they go to the next hole. When only one player "Aces" a hole, he or she wins it, and they move on to the next hole. In both cases the remaining putts are not putted out, leaving no negative consequence for first putts that are rolled too aggressively at speeds that are too high.

I've watched many games of Aces, and heard players say, "It teaches me to be aggressive and not leave putts short—at least they have a chance to go in." The problem, unfortunately, is that it teaches players to roll the ball *anywhere* past the hole, which is often not acceptable (too much speed creates too many lip-outs and too many three-putts).

There's a better way to learn to make more aces. Learn to roll your putts at the optimum speed as they approach the hole, so that they stop 17 inches past the hole when they miss. The games of the World Putting Championship (detailed in Chapter 4.8) are the best at teaching a "maximum aces" touch.

Putting to Extra-Small Holes

I've also heard golfers say that putting to an extra-small hole in a green (one that's less than the usual 4.25-inch diameter) helps them sharpen their focus on where they're aiming. While this may be true, it also ingrains a "putt-timidly" psyche into a golfer's touch system. It teaches golfers to die putts at the hole, because virtually the only way to hole a putt in a small hole is to roll it slowly enough for the ball to die into the cup. Putts that hit normal-sized holes at normal speeds tend to lip-out on the tighter radii of smaller cups.

The long-term results of putting to small holes are twofold: (1)

players instinctively learn to die their putts at the hole (instead of rolling them 17 inches past) and get too many putts that fall off-line because they roll so slowly; and (2) players learn to leave half of their putts short, with no chance of going in at all.

5.2
The Truth About Learning Aids

Some Learning Aids Are Worthless

Many golfers (73 percent, according to research from the National Golf Foundation) believe that learning aids don't work. That's a substantial majority, and how can so many golfers be wrong? It would make sense that when a majority is large, that majority must be right. To bolster this conclusion, the NGF says that about 40 percent of all golfers believe there are virtually no learning aids that are worth a flip—that all learning aids are gimmicks.

I've tested a lot of them, and let me assure you, I'm fully aware that many learning aids *are* worthless and *are* just gimmicks. And it's also true that even if a learning aid is great but is used in the wrong way, it offers no value to the user.

But . . . There Is Another Side to This Story

For more than thirty years, I've been using some excellent learning aids that provide meaningful feedback both to the students in our schools and in my personal teaching with tour professionals. I'm here to tell you (and I put my full reputation and credibility as a teaching professional behind this statement): **The right learning aid, used in the right way, can be a powerful teacher—and change your game!**

Immediate, accurate, and reliable feedback is essential to efficient learning. Most golfers try to improve their game on their own or with advice from buddies . . . and are patently unsuccessful. A good putting school, a good teaching professional who teaches putting, or a good learning aid that provides the feedback necessary for efficient learning are your best hopes for real improvement. Don't waste time practicing without one of them.

A Good Learning Aid— Used Properly— Makes a Difference

The key to getting true value from a learning aid is not only finding one that works properly, but finding one that provides useful feedback about the quality of your stroke or skill in the particular area where you need to change to improve. Remember, golfers' problems are usually unique to their own bodies and putting strokes (much like signatures and fingerprints), so each golfer needs the particular learning aid best designed to improve their unique problem.

For example, I struggled for years with left-to-right breaking putts and putting over terraces in greens. These particular problems are so important to me that I've had several SYNLawn putting greens installed in my own backyard (Figure 5.2-1).

Figure 5.2-1

These synthetic grass greens are made of nylon (see synlawngolf
.com for details); require no chemicals, water, or mowing; and provide true golf green performance for receiving shots. They also putt
beautifully. Not surprisingly, I had terraces, swales, and slopes built
into mine, and they accept chips, pitches, and full wedge shots as
well as the best bent and Bermuda "real" grass greens in the world.
But what I love most about them is that they're in my backyard and
provide me with easy access to game playing with feedback, so that
I can improve my putting.

To improve my left-to-right putting, I also use a Putting Track
and a Putting Tutor (Figure 5.2-2) . . .

Figure 5.2-2

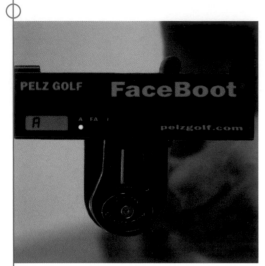

Figure 5.2-3

... to make sure I'm starting putts on-line, and I've recently added practice games with the Face Boot (Figure 5.2-3) for a few minutes three evenings a week (even when I'm traveling) to make sure my putterface angle is staying square through impact.

I've used many valuable learning aids with both my tour pro and school students. I've felt them work on my own game, I've seen them work in my schools, and I've personally witnessed tour pros improve their putting after using them.

Yes, 73 percent can be wrong.

While there *are* many poor learning aids and some *are* completely worthless, there are also some that are really valuable and really help. I've said it many times before and I'll continue to say it because it's true: A good learning aid, used properly to provide the proper feedback, is priceless to the learning process.

Practice does NOT make perfect! Practice makes permanent! If you practice and groove a poor putting stroke, you'll become a permanently poor putter, and you deserve it. Only good practice, with good feedback, will improve your putting.

Having said this, please don't think I'm writing this book to sell learning aids. That's crazy. I'm writing this book to give you the practice and putting-game information you need to improve your putting. Helping golfers make more putts and shoot lower scores is my life's work.

Many of our games can be played without learning aids, because the games themselves provide feedback on your putting. But for those of you who never want to use a learning aid on principle, please understand, you're making it tougher on yourself to improve.

I want to move on now and say one more thing before you start playing games, having fun, and becoming a better putter.

5.3
A Promise About Green-Reading

Knowing how much a putt is going to break before you putt is a terribly important aspect of putting. Not knowing where to aim to allow for break is a major problem. For years, I've studied why golfers read greens so poorly. I've also studied the problem of how to teach golfers to read greens better, and published extensively about this problem (*Dave Pelz's Putting Bible, 10 Minutes a Day to Better Putting,* the *Golf Magazine* cover story, "The Amazing Truth About Putting").

To summarize the results of my efforts to date: I've been very successful at showing and proving to golfers how poorly they read greens. I've been unsuccessful, however, at teaching them how to read greens correctly.

The following are facts:

1. Most golfers still consistently under-read how much their putts will break.
2. Most golfers allow for too little break in their putting setup and aim.
3. Most (approximately 90 percent) missed putts are missed *below* the hole.
4. After being shown how to aim perfectly, a golfer's subconscious compensations (established out of habit to compensate for his normal "too-low" aim) cause putts to miss *above* the hole rather than below it. These misses quickly drive them back to their old ways of playing too little break.
5. In summary, most golfers don't putt better after learning Nos. 1, 2, and 3 above, because subconscious compensations for this

problem are already built into their strokes, and these continue to occur even after I show them the perfect putting reads and aims.

So here is my current status on green-reading: I'm close to solving this problem. As this book goes to press, I'm deep into new research on the subject, and I've made a breakthrough discovery. I believe this new discovery will allow me to teach golfers to read greens quickly and correctly in the near future.

The data are not yet complete, and results are not yet ready to be published, but stay tuned. I'll reveal my secrets to reading greens in my next book. I promise!

O KAY, IT'S TIME TO START IMPROVING YOUR PUTTING.
In this chapter, let's walk through everything you need to
do in a serious program of playing games and having fun
to improve your ability to putt.

That sounds a bit odd, doesn't it: a serious program of playing
games and having fun? Can you have such a thing? Can you be serious (and work hard) while playing games and having fun?

Well . . . the answer is yes— and if you do it, your putting will
improve.

Here's the program. You should commit to playing these games
for at least fifteen minutes a night, three or four times a week, for
about a month. You can play them at home or at your golf course
practice putting green, by yourself or in competition with a friend,
and with or without the use of additional learning aids:

1. The first sixty to ninety minutes: Play and score the seven
   putting-performance games.
2. The next half hour: Evaluate your performance in the seven
   putting areas: Choose the games you'll need to play to improve
   your skills.
3. Over the next four weeks: Play the selected skill games for a
   minimum of thirty minutes in the evening, three times a week.
4. After four weeks: Spend another hour replaying and scoring the
   seven putting-performance games.
5. Reevaluate your putting weaknesses and choose new skill
   games to play for the next four weeks.

It's important that during this time you play at least one 18-hole
round each weekend, to let your improved putting skills work
smoothly into your game.

After four weeks, you should be putting better on the golf course, but you still need to continue. That's the program: cycle after cycle, playing seven performance games over and over, to continually reevaluate and identify the weakest area of your putting.

Now . . . let the games begin!

6.1
Play Seven "Performance" Games

Start now. Collect your putter, twelve balls, thirteen tees, a tablet, a pen, your 7-iron, and a tape measure in a small bag and proceed to a practice green. The better the putting green, the easier it will be to accomplish these games. It will take you approximately eight to ten minutes to set up, play, and score each of the seven performance games as detailed in Chapter 2. Remember to have a companion help you walk off and mark distances and write down scores. Allow at least an hour to complete all seven games.

You need all your scores in writing, because you'll never be able to remember them all. Take your putting performance data home and enter it on a Putting Performance Chart (either copy one from this book, Figure 6.1-1, or download it from www.pelzgolf.com /puttinggames). After completing your chart, you'll be able to realistically evaluate the strengths and weaknesses of your putting game.

PUTTING PERFORMANCE CHART

3' Putt Circle (misses)	6' Putt Circle (misses)	Makeable Putts (score)	Breaking Putts (score)	Intermediate Putts (score)	Lag Putts (score)	Lag Putts (remainder)	3-Putt Avoidance (# Putts)
- 12 -							- 60 -
						- 1000 -	
- 11 -	- 12 -				- 60 -		
						- 900 -	
- 10 -	- 11 -	- 60 -					- 50 -
- 9 -	- 10 -		- 60 -	- 60 -	- 50 -	- 800 -	
0	- 9 -	- 50 -				- 700 -	- 40 -
	- 8 -		- 50 -	- 50 -			
- 7 -					- 40 -	- 600 -	
- 6 -	- 7 -	- 40 -					- 30 -
	- 6 -		- 40 -	- 40 -		- 500 -	
- 5 -					- 30 -		
	- 5 -	- 30 -				- 400 -	
- 4 -			- 30 -				- 20 -
	- 4 -					- 300 -	
- 3 -	- 3 -				- 20 -		
		- 20 -	- 20 -	- 20 -		- 200 -	
- 2 -	- 2 -						
						- 100 -	
- 1 -	- 1 -					- 50 -	
- 0 -	- 0 -	- 12 -	- 12 -	- 12 -	- 12 -	- 0 -	- 12 -

Figure 6.1-1

Also remember that each twelve-putt game is only a snapshot of your true putting ability in that area of putting. You'll have bad days and good days. Recording your scores honestly will help you realize how your putting varies—as it does for all golfers—with your biorhythms, and averages out to your true putting skill level over the long haul.

6.2
Evaluate Your Putting Game

No one else has to see these numbers unless you want them to, although it's really fun to compete with friends over an entire golf season, based on these scores. Figures 6.2-1 A and 6.2-1B . . .

PUTTING PERFORMANCE CHART A

3′ Putt Circle (misses)	6′ Putt Circle (misses)	Makeable Putts (score)	Breaking Putts (score)	Intermediate Putts (score)	Lag Putts (score)	Lag Putts (remainder)	3-Putt Avoidance (# Putts)
- 12 -							- 60 -
						- 1000 -	
- 11 -	- 12 -				- 60 -		
						- 900 -	
- 10 -	- 11 -	- 60 -					- 50 -
- 9 -	- 10 -		- 60 -	- 60 -	- 50 -	- 800 -	
- 8 -	- 9 -	- 50 -				- 700 -	
	- 8 -		- 50 -	- 50 -			- 40 -
- 7 -					- 40 -	- 600 -	
	- 7 -	- 40 -					
- 6 -			- 40 -	- 40 -		- 500 -	- 30 -
	- 6 -						
- 5 -	- 5 -	- 30 -			- 30 -	- 400 -	
- 4 -	- 4 -		- 30 -			- 300 -	- 20 -
- 3 -	- 3 -	- 20 -			- 20 -	- 200 -	
- 2 -	- 2 -		- 20 -	- 20 -			
						- 100 -	
- 1 -	- 1 -					- 50 -	
- 0 -	- 0 -	- 12 -	- 12 -	- 12 -	- 12 -	- 0 -	- 12 -

Figure 6.2-1A

PRO PUTTING PERFORMANCE CHART B

3' Putt Circle (misses)	6' Putt Circle (misses)	Makeable Putts (score)	Breaking Putts (score)	Intermediate Putts (score)	Lag Putts (score)	Lag Putts (remainder)	3-Putt Avoidance (# Putts)
- 12 -							- 60 -
						- 1000 -	
- 11 -	- 12 -				- 60 -		
						- 900 -	
- 10 -	- 11 -	- 60 -					- 50 -
						- 800 -	
- 9 -	- 10 -		- 60 -	- 60 -	- 50 -		
						- 700 -	
- 8 -	- 9 -	- 50 -					- 40 -
	- 8 -		- 50 -	- 50 -			
- 7 -					- 40 -	- 600 -	
	- 7 -	- 40 -					
- 6 -						- 500 -	(30)
	- 6 -		- 40 -	- 40 -			
- 5 -					- 30 -	(428)	
	(5)	- 30 -				- 400 -	
- 4 -			- 30 -	(30)	(26)		- 20 -
	- 4 -					- 300 -	
- 3 -			(26)				
	- 3 -	- 20 -			- 20 -		
		(18)	- 20 -	- 20 -		- 200 -	
- 2 -	- 2 -						
(1.5)						- 100 -	
- 1 -	- 1 -						
						- 50 -	
- 0 -	- 0 -	- 12 -	- 12 -	- 12 -	- 12 -	- 0 -	- 12 -

Figure 6.2-1B

. . . show two Performance-Chart examples: the first sheet is full of numbers from a typical 20-handicap golfer, and the second shows the scoring of a typical PGA Tour player.

Obviously, there is a significant difference between the performance of a PGA Tour professional and a 20-handicap amateur. For this moment, let's assume that you're the 20-handicapper. Although the different performance games have different scoring metrics, the scoring is generally similar to the way you score when playing golf. The lower the score, the better the performance, and the higher the numbers, the worse your performance.

It becomes very simple to evaluate your relative strengths and weaknesses in these seven areas. After your first scores are entered, you'll see a one-day snapshot of your putting game. Your weakest area is identified by your worst performance, which is the tallest column on the page. In the opposite direction, your areas of strength are indicated by lower scores.

In this case the numbers indicate that you putted 3- and 6-footers well, and that your breaking-putt performance was pretty good, too. Your weakest areas (with the tallest columns) seem to be your intermediate and lag putting.

Always remember: Your Performance-Chart results for any one day, such as the one we just evaluated, are only a twelve-sample snapshot view of your putting. You will create additional snapshots every four to six weeks as you continue to play putting games and improve your putting in the evenings at home. For the long term your Summary Performance Sheet will look something like Figure 6.2-2 with each column height averaging your snapshot scores over time.

SUMMARY PUTTING PERFORMANCE GAME SCORES

Date:	3'	6'	Makeable	Breaking	Intermed.	Lag Score	Lag Remaind.	3-Putt Avoid.
6-15-2012	4	6	40	38	56	64	915	48
7-27-2015	6	10	32	22	44	64	902	42
9-2-2012	5	6	36	30	50	70	860	38
10-8-2012	7	7	30	36	50	60	783	40
11-6-2012	4	7	26	32	40	57	820	38
12-12-2012	4	9	22	30	48	52	800	40
1-6-2013	5	6	32	26	46	61	642	36
2-2-2013	3	7	26	30	42	55	660	33

Figure 6.2-2

Your Summary Performance Sheet will track your putting skills over time and provide an accurate overview of your entire putting game. It will clearly show where your putting has improved and identify the problem if your putting performance begins to slip in another area.

6.3
Play Skill Games in Your Weakest Skill Area

Play the Right Game

Now that you know the weakest area of your putting game is lag putting, you're ready to begin playing skill games to improve in that area. But which games should you play?

The Weakness vs. Skill Games table in Figure 6.3-1 below . . .

WEAKNESS vs. SKILL GAMES

Weakness Area	Skill Games to Play					
3' Circle	AIM	FACE ANGLE		IMPACT		SHORT
6' Circle	RHYTHM	AIM		FACE ANGLE		SHORT
Makeable	FEEL FOR SPEED		PREVIEW		MAKEABLE	FACE ANGLE
Breaking	FEEL FOR SPEED		MAKEABLE		PREVIEW	PATH
Intermediate	INTERMEDIATE		IMPACT		LAG	RHYTHM
LAG	IMPACT		PATH		LAG	INTERMEDIATE
3-Putt	LAG		RHYTHM		PATH	IMPACT

Figure 6.3-1

. . . identifies the skill games that are designed to improve play in the various areas of weakness. For example, if we continue to assume that the 20-handicapper's performance scores are indicative of your putting game, then the skill game you should play as your primary improvement focus is either the Impact Game (Chapter 3.4) or the Path Game (Chapter 3.2).

As you can see in Figure 6.3-1, each weakness area has its own set of four skill games designed to improve your performance. But because every golfer is unique, it's difficult to know in advance which game will improve your particular skill set most efficiently. We suggest you pick at least two of the four recommended skill games to play during the first few days of your improvement program. It is highly recommended that you play all four games at least a few times each (remember, they're only twelve-stroke games) within the first month.

The Most Difficult Game Is the Right One

Each of the four games listed for any one weakness area will focus your improvement on a skill vital to good putting. The game you find most difficult is the one you need to focus on the most. (Note: It may require multiple game scores to see a significant difference in your scoring abilities.)

The point is that you need to play these games to improve your putting. The more you play, the more improvement you'll see. Playing your worst (scoring) game over and over again to the various distances for thirty minutes is about the best evening practice you can achieve.

A word to the wise: Be smart and putt in practice like you're going to putt on the golf course. Make the same preview stroke before each real putting stroke, and take the same amount of time to putt in games at home, as you will for your most important putts on the course. Practice smart, play games smart, and play smart on the course: Let your mind and body perform the same so that you can optimize the carry-over from playing games at home to playing rounds on the course.

6.4
Play 18 Holes Every Weekend

You should play at least one 18-hole round every weekend while you're playing putting games at home in the evenings, to let your improvement work its way into your game on the course. Even if you think you're practicing the same as you play, it's difficult to exactly duplicate at home both the physical and mental gymnastics you have to go through on the golf course.

Do the best you can: Be sure to play games at home using the same rituals and timing as you employ on-course, to help your improvements transfer to your on-course putting as efficiently as possible. Then also play 18 holes often enough to complete the job, letting those improved skills transfer completely and smoothly (so you don't even have to think about them) into your on-course performance.

6.5
Recycle: Repeat Your
Performance Games

It's time to recycle.

Four weeks into your putting-game program, let's imagine that you've been playing the Impact Game and the Lag-Touch Game three evenings a week, and that your scores have been improving (although they're still somewhat erratic). A month (no longer than six weeks) of work on any particular skill is a good period of time, after which you should recycle and reevaluate whether your lag-putting performance is still the weakest part of your putting.

To determine this, play the Seven Performance Games again, and record your scores on the practice green and take them home to enter on your Performance Chart. Such reevaluation is one part of this putting-game program that I really enjoy. It's fun to retest and see the relative weaknesses and strengths in your putting game over time.

It's Easy After the First Time

Once you know the games and how to set them up quickly and efficiently, it's all about the putting and seeing if you can perform better than in the past. I'm telling you, when you see your performance improving and your scores going down, it's exciting to internalize this fact: You *really are* becoming a better putter.

So do it. By following the improvement program in this book, you'll see one weak area in your putting improve after another. Then it will be time to work on yet another weak area. Can you imagine how your putting will improve if you stay on this program for years, and keep improving the weakest area of your putting as time goes by? It's an exciting prospect, and I hope you achieve it.

6.6
Let Us Know How You're Doing

As your game scores improve, your putting will improve. By playing putting games at home in the evenings and 18-hole rounds on the weekends, you *will* improve your putting. In fact, if you play the games, follow the rules, and reevaluate your skills often enough, you can't help but improve. I've done it myself and I've seen it work for my students. And one of the neat things about it: You have fun while you're doing it.

The more quality feedback you receive during your games, the more efficiently your improvement will come. And believe it or not, the more accurately you keep track of your scores and improvement, the more consistently your improvement will continue. For this reason we'd like you to keep in touch with us.

It's Easy to Watch the Improvement

We'll make it easy for you to keep track of your Skill Game improvements and your periodic Performance Test scores by inviting you to enter them on our website. We've reserved a special place on our website for our friends (you're our friend if you're working to improve your putting) to keep track of their putting games. It's free, it's easy, and you have your choice of keeping your scores and progress private or allowing your friends to see your data.

If you log on to www.pelzgolf.com and register your name and information, we'll give you your own Putting Performance Evaluation Sheet and Skill Game scoring logbook. Keeping track of your putting progress over time then becomes easy, because you can quickly enter your game scores with a few strokes on your computer keyboard. Your own personal Putting Performance Chart will always show you the latest status of your putting game, and your progress (or lack thereof) toward improving it.

Again let me emphasize: We will keep all information and scores private, or let your friends see them at your discretion. We simply want to make it easy for you to keep track of, and see, the improvement in your putting game.

Keep in Touch

So please keep in touch one way or another and let us know of your progress. We would of course enjoy seeing your Skill Game and Performance Game scores, and any comments you care to share with us as to your own improvement or how we can improve the program.

If you have new and better games, or different ways to help golfers improve their putting, we would like to see that, too. And above all: Have fun playing our putting games and holing more putts on the golf course. If you don't have time to play putting games at home, don't beat yourself up or worry about your putting . . . just enjoy golf anyway. Because it's a great game—and a great way to enjoy life!

Good Putting to You—

Dave Pelz

DAVE PELZ

DRIVING PRINCIPLES

The driving principles of our putting games are as follows:

- To accurately measure a golfer's putting performance in seven distinct areas of putting (Chapter 2) so that he or she can identify areas of weakness in their putting game.
- To provide games that give feedback to golfers, relative to stroke mechanics (Chapter 3), to help them improve their putting.
- To provide games that give feedback to golfers involving their mind's eye, feel, and touch (Chapter 4), to improve their putting.

PUTT SPEED

The detail for measuring putt speed is as follows:

- The speed at which a ball rolls determines the amount of break in any breaking putt. The faster a putt rolls, the less it breaks. The slower it rolls, the more it breaks.
- The speed at which a ball approaches a hole is critical to good putting. Putt approach speed is measured by how far the ball rolls short of or past the hole when it misses the cup.
- The optimum putt speed is that which gives the ball the maximum chance of both hitting and staying in the hole. This

speed has been measured to carry a ball 17 inches past the back edge of the cup if it does not hit the hole or go in.

- Teaching golfers to roll putts on average 17 inches past the hole is best accomplished by having them play games that reward putts that roll past the back edge of the hole, but no farther than 34 inches past, into an area called the "good" zone (Figure Appendix A-1).

Figure
Appendix
A-1

- Games that measure putt miss-distance from optimum speed do so by comparing a putt's actual roll distance to the perfect roll distance for an optimum speed putt (perfect roll distance = target distance + $2\frac{1}{8}$ inches + 17 inches (Figure Appendix A-2).

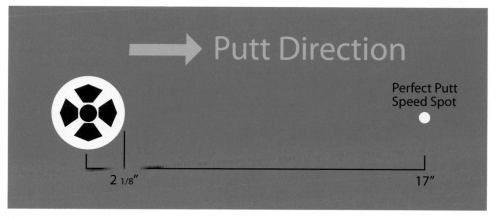

Figure
Appendix
A-2

- Miss-speed is equated to miss-distance of a putt's roll, as measured by the difference between its actual and the perfect roll distance (Figure Appendix A-3).

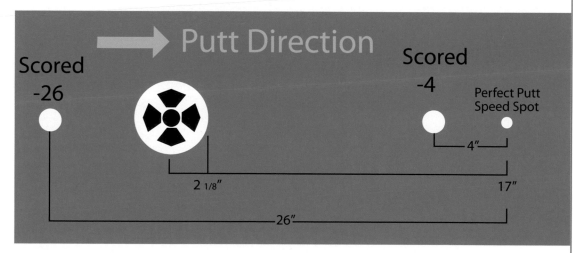

Figure
Appendix
A-3

• Putts that hit the hole and lip-out more than 90 degrees to stop in front of the hole's back edge, are considered in the "good" zone if they come to rest within 34 inches of the closest edge of the hole (Figure Appendix A-4).

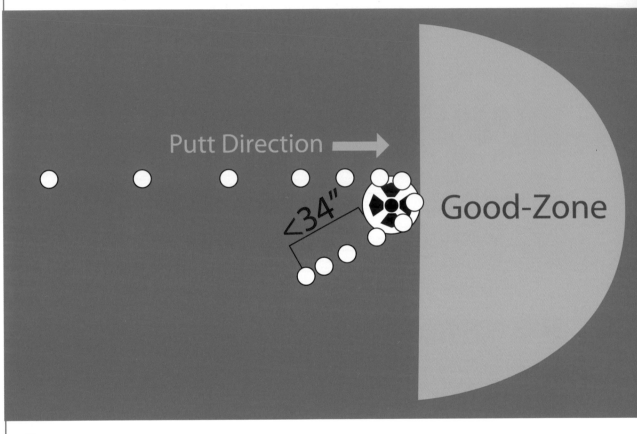

Figure
Appendix
A-4

FORGET PUTTING MECHANICS AND GO PLAY

Once you practice and groove improvements enough to make a habit of them, you're ready to forget them and go play golf on the course. Great putters don't think about their strokes when they play. They make good strokes out of habit, while their mind's eye focuses on reading the green and dialing in their touch to match the speed of their putts to the break they read.

CHANGE TAKES TIME AND ENERGY

Here's a question to consider: Should you: (1) refine and improve the putting stroke you have, (2) make major changes and then rebuild, or (3) start from scratch and develop an all-new putting stroke?

Many students in our Dave Pelz Scoring Game Schools ask this question, and it's a good one. To answer this question for yourself, I recommend you consider the following:

- The longer the time and the greater the efforts you've put into building the putting stroke that you have now, the more difficult it will be to start over. Old habits die hard. It's one thing to improve the well-grooved putting stroke that you've used for years by tweaking it. It's another thing entirely to forget all of your old habits and start over.
- This decision also depends on what the lifetime goal for your golf game is, and how much time and energy you have available to put into achieving that goal. Many good players who aren't satisfied with their putting and decide to start over end up in "no-man's-land," victims of circumstances (life tends to get in the way) that don't allow them to finish the job.
- If you don't have enough time to form new habits (and forget old habits by burying them under many thousands of new repetitions), don't start over.

So the answer for most golfers is pretty clear: Improve what you have to the best of your ability—don't start from scratch. If you have ten to twenty minutes a day, three or four days a week, you can make significant improvements in your putting in just a few months. If you think this kind of commitment is in your wheelhouse, commit to it and go for it. It will allow you to enjoy your game to the max.

If you don't have at least ten minutes a day several times a week, then you should stop worrying about your putting altogether and enjoy your game as it is. Only in the rare case when you have several hours a day to work on putting should you consider starting over.

TEST BEFORE YOU GROOVE

Having said the above, there is one test you might want to run before expending a significant effort to improve your putting. You may well benefit from testing belly, long, and "lead-hand-low" putting techniques before you start the putting-improvement program described in this book.

I suggest this based on data I've tabulated from my schools, which shows that many golfers hole a significantly higher percentage of putts inside of twelve feet with one of these three putting methods than they do with their conventional putting stroke. While none of the three techniques is a panacea for perfect putting, each has an advantage over conventional putting for some golfers.

Never forget: Your mind tells your body how to swing the putter, and the putter tells the ball where and how fast to roll during the impact of your putting stroke. That's what you control—your green-reading (where you aim) and how you swing your putter through impact.

THE TEST IS SIMPLE

You can easily test the previously mentioned putting techniques as follows:

(Note: Try not to change your grip during these tests. Your goal is to play three different putting games putting four different ways, comparing your results with belly, long, and lead-hand-low techniques to your conventional grip and putting motion. If you play three different games for three days in a row, your putting results will prove which putting technique provides the best results for you.)

Play these three performance games each day, once with each putting technique, as follows:

1. 3-Foot-Circle Game (see Chapter 2.1: Page 17)
2. Makeable-Putt Game (see Chapter 2.3: Page 27)
3. Lag-Putt Game (see Chapter 2.6: Page 42)

If the same technique wins each day for all three games, your decision is simple: Switch your putting to that technique. Then start the improvement program described in this book and try to improve your putting even further over time.

If your results are mixed, then retest until one technique stands out above the rest in both scoring and comfort. In some cases you'll see clear results that tell you that one technique is better for short putts while a different technique is better for long putts. In this case, I recommend you work on improving both techniques in their winning area, and play with two putters in your bag (take a long iron out of your bag—you won't miss it).

T**HE AUTHORS WOULD LIKE TO THANK SUMMIT ROCK CLUB** at Horseshoe Bay, Texas, for their cooperation and help in making their fine facilities available for use in this book.

We also thank Phil Mickelson for allowing us to show how he plays some of the games in this book, as he prepares for his play on the PGA Tour, and our instruction staff—Ty, Trent, Marc, Stefan, Ben, Peter, and David—for helping develop and test the learning aids in our schools.

In addition, we also thank Sven Nilson for his photographic skills and graphical presentations used herein.